GROUP TREATMENT MANUAL FOR PERSISTENT DEPRESSION

This Cognitive Behavioral Analysis System of Psychotherapy (CBASP) Group Manual is a treatment guide for mental health professionals working with persistently depressed individuals. The manual provides a clear step-by-step application of CBASP as a group treatment modality, the research findings supporting the effectiveness of this treatment, and suggested methods of assessing outcome as well as possible applications or adaptations of the treatment to different settings and disorders. This manual is accompanied by a separate workbook for patients.

Liliane Sayegh, Ph.D., is a clinical psychologist specialized in mood disorders at the Douglas Mental Health University Institute, Montreal, Quebec, Canada. She is also an assistant professor in the Department of Psychology at McGill University.

J. Kim Penberthy, Ph.D., ABPP, is a board certified clinical psychologist and professor of psychiatry and neurobehavioral sciences at the University of Virginia School of Medicine. She is the Director for Research at the UVA Contemplative Sciences Center as well as the Co-Director of the Effective Communication and Coping Skills for Physicians and Physician Clinical Evaluation Programs at UVA.

GROUP TREATMENT MANUAL FOR PERSISTENT DEPRESSION

COGNITIVE BEHAVIORAL
ANALYSIS SYSTEM OF
PSYCHOTHERAPY (CBASP)

THERAPIST'S GUIDE

Liliane Sayegh

J. Kim Penberthy

First published 2016
by Routledge
711 Third Avenue, New York, NY 10017

and by Routledge
2 Park Square, Milton Park, Abingdon, Oxon, OX14 4RN

Routledge is an imprint of the Taylor & Francis Group, an informa business

© 2016 Taylor & Francis

The rights of Liliane Sayegh and J. Kim Penberthy to be identified as authors of this work have been asserted by them in accordance with sections 77 and 78 of the Copyright, Designs and Patents Act 1988.

All rights reserved. The purchase of this copyright material confers the right on the purchasing institution to photocopy pages which bear the photocopy icon and copyright line at the bottom of the page. No other parts of this book may be reprinted or reproduced or utilised in any form or by any electronic, mechanical, or other means, now known or hereafter invented, including photocopying and recording, or in any information storage or retrieval system, without permission in writing from the publishers.

Trademark notice: Product or corporate names may be trademarks or registered trademarks, and are used only for identification and explanation without intent to infringe.

Library of Congress Cataloging in Publication Data
Names: Sayegh, Liliane, author. | Penberthy, J. Kim, author.
Title: Group treatment manual for persistent depression : cognitive behavioral analysis system of psychotherapy (CBASP) therapist's guide / by Liliane Sayegh and J. Kim Penberthy.
Description: New York, NY : Routledge, 2016.
Includes bibliographical references and index.
Identifiers: LCCN 2015035159| ISBN 9781138926004 (hbk : alk. paper) | ISBN 9781138926011 (pbk : alk. paper) | ISBN 9781315683317 (ebk)
Subjects: LCSH: Depression, Mental—Treatment—Handbooks, manuals, etc. | Cognitive therapy—Handbooks, manuals, etc.
Classification: LCC RC537 .S298 2016
DDC 616.85/270651—dc23
LC record available at http://lccn.loc.gov/2015035159

ISBN: 978-1-138-92600-4 (hbk)
ISBN: 978-1-138-92601-1 (pbk)
ISBN: 978-1-315-68331-7 (ebk)

Typeset in Dutch823 BT
by Keystroke, Station Road, Codsall, Wolverhampton

CONTENTS

FOREWORD ix

PREFACE xi

ACKNOWLEDGMENTS xiii

PART I INTRODUCTION 1

PERSISTENT DEPRESSION 1
INTERPERSONAL CHARACTERISTICS OF THE PERSISTENTLY DEPRESSED
   PATIENT 2
CBASP HISTORY 4
CBASP RESEARCH EVIDENCE 5
GROUP-CBASP APPROACH 6
GROUP-CBASP RESEARCH EVIDENCE 9

**PART II GROUP-CBASP METHODOLOGY AND
PROCEDURE 13**

SELECTION CRITERIA 14
TRAINING FOR CLINICIANS 15
THE SIGNIFICANT OTHER HISTORY (SOH) EXERCISE AND TRANSFERENCE
   HYPOTHESIS (TH)—*FORMS 3 TO 5* 16
THE SITUATIONAL ANALYSIS (SA) (COPING SURVEY QUESTIONNAIRE)
   WITHIN A GROUP SETTING 20
DISCIPLINED PERSONAL INVOLVEMENT (DPI) 21
THE INTERPERSONAL DISCRIMINATION EXERCISE (IDE) 22
CONTINGENT PERSONAL RESPONSIVITY (CPR) 23
GROUP-CBASP SESSIONS OUTLINE 24

PART III GROUP-CBASP SESSIONS 25

GROUP-CBASP SESSIONS 1–20 25

GROUP-CBASP: SESSION 1 27

PRESENTATIONS, ROLES OF GROUP MEMBERS AND GROUP LEADER 28
Group Members' Role 28
Group Leader's Role 28
DEPRESSION—*FORMS 1 & 2* 28
COST OF DEPRESSION 29
CHARTING MOOD—*HANDOUT 2* 29

GROUP-CBASP: SESSION 2 31

THE INTERPERSONAL DOMAIN—*HANDOUT 3* 32
***HANDOUT 3: YOUR INTERPERSONAL DOMAIN* 33**
THE CYCLE OF DEPRESSION AND INACTIVITY 34

GROUP-CBASP: SESSION 3 35

**MALADAPTIVE COGNITIVE AND COPING STRATEGIES OF PERSISTENTLY
DEPRESSED PATIENTS—*HANDOUT 6* 36**
***HANDOUT 6: THE CYCLE OF HOPELESSNESS AND POWERLESSNESS
LEADS TO PERSISTENT DEPRESSION* 38**
THE SITUATIONAL ANALYSIS (SA) ADAPTED TO A GROUP MODALITY 39
ELICITATION PHASE OF THE SITUATIONAL ANALYSIS (SA)—*HANDOUT 9* 39
***HANDOUT 9: THE SITUATIONAL ANALYSIS (SA) (FOR GROUP THERAPY)* 44**

GROUP-CBASP: SESSION 4 47

REMEDIATION PHASE OF THE SITUATIONAL ANALYSIS (SA)—*HANDOUT 10* 48
***HANDOUT 10: SITUATIONAL ANALYSIS (SA): REMEDIATION PHASE* 50**
USING A FUTURE SITUATIONAL ANALYSIS (SA)—*HANDOUT 11* 51

GROUP-CBASP: SESSION 5 52

**PRACTICING THE SITUATIONAL ANALYSIS (SA) WITH ELICITATION AND
REMEDIATION PHASES 52**

GROUP-CBASP: SESSION 6 53

***HANDOUT 12: YOUR INTERPERSONAL DOMAIN* 54**

GROUP-CBASP: SESSIONS 7 & 8 58

**PRACTICING THE SITUATIONAL ANALYSIS (SA) WITH ELICITATION AND
REMEDIATION PHASES 58**

GROUP-CBASP: SESSIONS 9 & 10 59

**THE INTERPERSONAL CIRCUMPLEX IN GROUP-CBASP—*HANDOUTS
13, 14 & 19* 60**
***HANDOUT 19: EIGHT STYLES OF INTERPERSONAL RELATING* 63**

GROUP-CBASP: SESSIONS 11 & 12 65

USING AN INTERPERSONAL PROFILE IN GROUP-CBASP 66

GROUP-CBASP: SESSIONS 13 & 14 68

COMPLEMENTARY AND NON-COMPLEMENTARY INTERACTIONS 69
UNDERSTANDING YOUR INTERPERSONAL PROBLEMS AND PROFILE ON
THE INTERPERSONAL CIRCUMPLEX—*HANDOUT 16* 70
*HANDOUT 16: YOUR INTERPERSONAL PROFILE: HOW CAN IT HELP GET
WHAT YOU WANT?* 73
EXAMPLES OF CONTINGENT PERSONAL RESPONSIVITY (CPR) IN
GROUP-CBASP 74
Case Example 1 74
Case Example 2 76

GROUP-CBASP: SESSIONS 15 & 16 79

PUTTING IT ALL TOGETHER 80
YOUR INTERPERSONAL PROFILE 80

GROUP-CBASP: SESSIONS 17 TO 20 82

TERMINATION 83
GROUP-CBASP MAINTENANCE AND FOLLOW-UP FOR RELAPSE
PREVENTION 84
ETHICAL CONSIDERATIONS FOR GROUP-CBASP 84

PART IV ASSESSING CHANGE IN GROUP-CBASP 85

MEASURING SKILLS ACQUISITION IN GROUP-CBASP 85
The Self-Administered Interpersonal Discrimination Exercise (IDE)—*Form 7* 85
The Personal Questionnaire (PQ) 86
The Patient Performance Rating Form (PPRF)—*Form 8* 87
ASSESSING INTERPERSONAL DISPOSITIONS IN PERSISTENT DEPRESSION—
FORMS 9 & 10, HANDOUTS 13 & 14 87

APPENDICES 91

FORM 1: DO YOU HAVE MAJOR DEPRESSION? 92
FORM 2: DO YOU HAVE PERSISTENT DEPRESSIVE DISORDER (DYSTHYMIA)? 93
HANDOUT 2: MOOD CHART 94
FORM 3: CBASP SIGNIFICANT OTHER HISTORY 96
FORM 4: CBASP INTERPERSONAL QUESTIONNAIRE (CIQ) 98
FORM 5: CBASP INTERPERSONAL QUESTIONNAIRE (CIQ)—ADMINISTRATION
AND SCORING 100
FORM 6: CASE EXAMPLE OF ALICE 101
HANDOUT 17: THE SITUATIONAL ANALYSIS (SA) (FOR INDIVIDUAL
THERAPY) 109
HANDOUT 9: THE SITUATIONAL ANALYSIS (SA) (FOR GROUP THERAPY) 111
HANDOUT 18: THE SITUATIONAL ANALYSIS (SA) (ONE-PAGE FORM) 115
HANDOUT 11: FUTURE SITUATIONAL ANALYSIS (SA) 116
HANDOUT 10: SITUATIONAL ANALYSIS (SA): REMEDIATION PHASE 117
FORM 7: FORM FOR SCORING THE SELF-ADMINISTERED INTERPERSONAL
DISCRIMINATION EXERCISE (SAD-IDE) 118
FORM 8: PATIENT PERFORMANCE RATING FORM (PPRF) FOR SITUATIONAL
ANALYSIS (SA) 119
FORM 9: CIRCUMPLEX MEASURES 121
FORM 10: NORMS FOR THE CIRCUMPLEX SCALE OF INTERPERSONAL
VALUES (CSIV)/NORMS FOR THE CIRCUMPLEX SCALE OF INTERPERSONAL
EFFICACY (CSIE) 122

VIII CONTENTS

HANDOUT 13: YOUR INTERPERSONAL CIRCUMPLEX—VALUES/MOTIVES 123
HANDOUT 14: YOUR INTERPERSONAL CIRCUMPLEX—EFFICACY 124

REFERENCES 125

INDEX 133

FOREWORD

Teaching therapists to treat patients with Persistent Depressive Disorder (PDD) is always a difficult undertaking. The main reason is that these patients do not think, emote, or behave like their psychotherapists. Many persistently depressed patients, although fully competent intellectually, may function emotionally on a level that resembles the preoperational functioning of children (Piaget, 1926). This means that clinicians, before they can adequately address the patients' problems, must first learn to do the following: (1) take seriously the impaired functioning of these individuals, and significantly modify their perception of patients who are sitting with them in the room; (2) adjust their expectations of what patients can do (at the outset of treatment) and help facilitate felt emotional safety for the patient; and (3) learn to think in acquisition learning terms regarding what patients learn from their therapy work over time.

Practitioners who will be taught to administer the *CBASP Group Treatment Manual for Persistent Depression* must learn to master the above three practitioner learning goals before they are able to administer Group-CBASP. Group-CBASP delineates specific learning goals for the patients throughout each session. The manual specifies how patient learning will be acquired as participants process through the 20 group sessions; ultimately, clinicians will be taught how to determine the extent of patient learning and more importantly, to determine how patient learning has modified the depressive symptoms as well as the PDD of their individual group members.

Group-CBASP training for therapists will be challenging and enlightening. In short, therapist training will be difficult but certainly achievable based on the way the *Group Treatment Manual* is delineated. The session tasks are described thoroughly and clearly and the format throughout should stimulate the asking of relevant questions and produce lively discussions that will deepen the understanding of the goals of CBASP.

The *CBASP Group Treatment Manual for Persistent Depression* should prepare training therapists for the arduous task of addressing effectively the unique problems PDD patients bring to us.

James P. McCullough, Jr.
Professor of Psychology & Psychiatry
Department of Psychology
Virginia Commonwealth University
Richmond, Virginia

REFERENCE

Piaget, J. (1926). *The Language and Thought of the Child.* New York: Harcourt, Brace. (Original work published in 1923.)

PREFACE

Depression is a debilitating illness and has the power to unravel and to undermine an individual's ambitions, life, health, and goals. The long-term consequences of misdiagnosed or untreated depression are known to be devastating, leading to under-functioning or nonfunctioning individuals, impoverished social and professional interactions, and sometimes to broken homes, ruined relationships, or the death of the individual. Depression is indeed a challenge to the sufferer who struggles to acknowledge, accept, and battle with his or her mood disorder. Depression is also a challenge to mental health professionals, family physicians, and care providers, family members and close friends of the sufferer, some of whom may feel shut-out, powerless, and inadequate when they intervene to try and help or offer support.

We undertook the writing of this manual with the primary purpose of sharing with other mental health professionals what we have found to be an empowering and effective therapeutic approach for helping individuals diagnosed with persistent depression. Cognitive Behavioral Analysis System of Psychotherapy (CBASP) is an engaging interpersonal therapy that, when set in the context of a group approach, overpowers and disarms the grip of depression by breaking the silence and the isolation that each sufferer feels trapped within. We have repeatedly witnessed both therapists and group members in Group-CBASP develop a supportive environment where each member is invested in understanding and helping others with their struggles as well as their own. This group dynamic belongs to its members, they appropriate the space and create a place where their voices are heard and matter. CBASP has given us the theoretical and clinical framework within which to work and it is up to the therapist to engage each sufferer in a way that is respectful and meaningful and that models commitment and involvement throughout group therapy. Such dynamic involvement is contagious to others in the group who are pulled into the collaborative effort toward change. Learning goes around the table and is reciprocal; I learn from the sufferer, he or she learns from other sufferers, and sufferers learn from me. We can only be transformed by the experience of Group-CBASP when learning is not acquired didactically but rather is built through the use of concrete CBASP exercises and therapeutic strategies introduced by an invested and engaged therapist. The best way, in our opinion, to loosen the grip of persistent depression is to understand that patients can engage their own process of self-healing but will do this best when also engaging others in reciprocal interactions.

We are both indebted to Dr. James P. McCullough Jr. who devoted his life's work to the development of CBASP and to the relief of the agony and suffering associated with Persistent Depressive Disorder. He is a true pioneer in the effective treatment of this chronic and debilitating disorder and we have him to thank for the current adaptation to group format.

Liliane Sayegh, Montreal, Quebec, Canada
J. Kim Penberthy, Charlottesville, VA, USA

ACKNOWLEDGMENTS

We are very grateful for the collaboration and continued guidance of Dr. James P. McCullough, Jr., Professor of Psychology and Psychiatry at Virginia Commonwealth University in Richmond, Virginia. Jim developed CBASP to help chronically depressed patients whom he saw were not responding to other empirically based psychotherapies. Jim continues to research, teach, and implement CBASP and was crucial in our development of a group application of this powerful and life-changing psychotherapy.

We are also grateful for the collaboration of Dr. Kenneth D. Locke, Professor at the Department of Psychology and Communication Studies, University of Idaho, for his continual assistance in helping us translate the circumplex model into a useful clinical tool, for his participation in the research aspect of the project, and for draft reviews. Most of all, we need to acknowledge him for the circumplex scales he developed that have permitted the link to be made between the importance of one's values and perceived efficacy regarding particular interpersonal situations and achieving a Desired Outcome in that specific interpersonal situation as demonstrated by the CBASP model. Our research has indeed confirmed Professor Locke's findings that people are likely to engage in activities if they feel more confident in their ability to do so, which they have an opportunity to develop in Group-CBASP.

Many thanks are also extended to Mr. John Swan, our colleague at the International CBASP Society (Scottish Division) and friend, whose sharp clinical eyes have perused the pages of this manual. Thanks also to Anna-Majia Kokko, psychologist and CBASP trainer in Finland, who invited us to teach Group-CBASP in Finland and inspired us to formalize the manuals, thus helping to spark this project. We are also grateful for the help received from Sybille Saury in the painstaking work of editing. Special thanks go to our wonderful illustrator, Morgan Yi, whose lovely images add so much to our workbooks. Our effort is truly an international collaboration!

It is important to recognize the contribution of many graduate psychology students who have contributed over the past eight years to the development of the group manual with their feedback, ideas, and conceptualizations while they were co-therapists learning Group-CBASP and some of them to the research aspects of Group-CBASP. Thank you to Elena Saimon's impeccable research assistance and to Hélène Thériault, Psy.D.; Ariane Lazaridès, Ph.D.; Leechen Farkas-Zukor, Ph.D.; Joëlle Jobin, Ph.D. candidate; Charlotte Weber, Ph.D. and Olivia Beaulieu-Denault, Ph.D. candidate. Thank you to the exceptional psychology post-doctoral fellows who have collaborated on research and have worked hard to learn the art and science of CBASP: Christopher Gioia, Ph.D., Andrea Konig, Ph.D., Michelle Vaughan, Ph.D., Jennifer Wartella, Ph.D., and J. Nile Wagley, Ph.D. Thank you also to additional collaborators on research including the excellent statistical work of Joshua Hook, Ph.D. and research collaboration with Sarah Meshberg-Cohen, Ph.D., Aaron Martin, Ph.D., and Stephanie Cockrell, MSW.

I (Sayegh) extend my special thanks to my family (my husband Jim and children Elisabeth and Paul) for their support and for believing in the value of this project both clinically and personally for me.

I (Penberthy) also extend sincere thanks to my husband David and daughter J. Morgan Penberthy, for their cheerful and unwavering support throughout this process—I could not have completed this important project without them!

Most of all, we thank our patients, without whom none of this would be possible. Ultimately, this work is dedicated to all of those who suffer from persistent and chronic depression. Our desired outcome is for our work to help alleviate your suffering and promote healing.

Liliane Sayegh, Montreal, Quebec, Canada
J. Kim Penberthy, Charlottesville, VA, USA

PART

I

INTRODUCTION

PERSISTENT DEPRESSION

Persistent or chronic depression is a serious and debilitating disease that impacts hundreds of millions of people worldwide. Persistent depression differs from acute or single-episode depression in multiple ways, including symptom profiles, hypothesized aetiologies, and effective treatment approaches. This manual is designed to teach a group format of Cognitive Behavioral Analysis System of Psychotherapy (CBASP), which is designed specifically to treat the persistently depressed patient.

DSM-5 (APA, 2013) has consolidated the DSM-IV categories of Chronic Major Depressive Disorder and Dysthymic Disorder into one category called Persistent Depressive Disorder. To be called Persistent Depressive Disorder, the depressive symptoms must be of at least two years' duration, as previously indicated for chronic major depression. The addition of a specifier is suggested to indicate whether the Persistent Depressive Disorder is a "pure" dysthymic syndrome; a double depression, which is a major depression superimposed on dysthymia; a recurrent major depression with residual symptoms between episodes; or is a major depressive disorder lasting for two years or more without remission (APA, 2013). Major depression is the most common mental health disorder with a lifetime prevalence rate of over 16 percent (Kessler et al., 2003) and is the leading cause of disability worldwide, as well as a major contributor to the global burden of disease (World Federation for Mental Health, 2012, 2015). According to the NIMH Collaborative Depressive Study, about 20 percent of patients with major depressive disorder will develop a chronic course of the illness (Keller et al., 1984). Patients with recurrent depression are also at risk of developing a more chronic picture with each new episode of depression (Keller & Boland, 1998). DSM-5 added a severity specifier to determine the degree of functional disability in persistent depression (APA, 2013).

Numerous patients (up to 15 percent) remain very depressed after multiple interventions with aggressive pharmacological and psychotherapeutic treatments (Berlim & Turecki, 2007). Only about 20 percent to 40 percent of patients receiving their first treatment for a major depressive episode are expected to achieve a relatively asymptomatic state (Sackeim, 2001). Even then, there is often a lag until a full recovery of social and occupational functioning is achieved (Sackeim, 2001). It is common to find that patients who respond to treatment can continue to experience residual attenuated depressive symptoms as well as symptoms not usually considered among the core symptoms of depression. These symptoms may include irritability, problems with depressive thinking, and problems functioning socially and at work (Fava, Ruini, & Belaise, 2007).

Persistent depression has been found to be associated with a younger age of onset, a family history of mood disorders, co-morbid anxiety, substance abuse, and personality disorders (Hölzel, Härter, Reese, & Kriston, 2011; Kornstein & Schneider, 2001; Sonawalla & Fava, 2001; Thase, 1997; Thase, Friedman, & Howland, 2001). In addition, patients with persistent depression have more problems within the social environment (e.g. low social integration, low social support, negative social interaction) (Hölzel et al., 2011).

McCullough (2000) stresses the distinction between early-onset (depression before the age of 21) and late-onset patients (depression at or after the age of 21) that has been proposed by Akiskal et al. (1981, 1980). This distinction was substantiated by evidence that the majority (72 percent) of patients with dysthymic disorder have an early onset of symptoms. Early-onset patients also have an earlier onset of a major depressive disorder with a longer index of a major depressive episode, which suggests a more severe condition (Klein et al., 1999). McCullough describes the early-onset depressives as frequently having developmental histories characterized by psychological insults or psychological/emotional trauma or maltreatment. These patients were found to respond more effectively to psychotherapy (CBASP) with or without medication, while late-onset patients without childhood maltreatment or trauma appeared to respond better to combination treatment (medication and CBASP) (Nemeroff et al., 2003).

INTERPERSONAL CHARACTERISTICS OF THE PERSISTENTLY DEPRESSED PATIENT

CBASP is based upon an interpersonal theory of psychosocial functioning and thus understanding the role of interpersonal functioning in persistently depressed individuals is critical. As stated, early-onset persistently depressed individuals frequently present with a history of early trauma, maltreatment, abuse, or having experienced repeated psychological insults (Dube et al., 2001; Heim & Nemeroff, 2001; Kendler et al., 1995). In the CBASP model, these insults are hypothesized to lead to feelings of not being emotionally safe and not trusting others (resulting from classical or Pavlovian conditioning with a hurtful other) (McCullough, Schramm, & Penberthy, 2014) as well as social withdrawal and avoidance behaviors (resulting from operant or Skinnerian conditioning) and subsequent developmental arrest which negatively impacts social, cognitive, and emotional growth in disastrous ways (McCullough, 2000, 2006; McCullough et al., 2014). McCullough (2000) previously described what the cognitive-emotional derailment that accrues from the childhood interpersonal retreat looks like; he labeled it *preoperational functioning* borrowing the developmental phrase from Piaget (Piaget, 1926). The *preoperational* adult patient who is chronically depressed is hypothesized to function at a cognitive-emotional level resembling that of a preoperational child. Pre-causal thinking and jumping from a premise to a conclusion about reality characterize the thought processes of many persistently depressed patients. Conversing in a monologue style and not being informed by the behavior of others is another characteristic of the individual functioning at a preoperational level of thinking. Finally, pervasive ego-centricity and being unable to generate empathy with others consigns the person to a solitary existence. All areas of social endeavor for this adult can become severely limited over time and lead to the hallmark symptoms of chronic depression: *helplessness and hopelessness.*

The CBASP model posits that persistently depressed individuals become rigid in their interpersonal functioning. The previously mentioned preoperational level of functioning (Piaget, 1926, 1981) renders these patients unable to estimate the interpersonal consequences of their behavior, unable to critically appraise feedback, or to deduce causal relationships prospectively. Such deficits keep the chronically depressed individual perceptually disconnected from the environment, leaving the person feeling defeated, wary of interpersonal involvement, and without a sense of agency to act upon the world. According to the CBASP model, the cognitive-emotional functioning of chronically depressed individuals manifests interpersonally as both hostile detachment and excessive submissiveness along with an inability to move out of this interpersonal stance, even in response to friendly or supportive others. Unable to attach empathically to others or to assert themselves effectively, chronically depressed individuals have difficulty meeting their interpersonal needs; a deficit that purportedly maintains a cycle of primitive cognitive and interpersonal functioning and long-standing depressed mood (McCullough, 2000). Although acutely depressed individuals may also have interpersonal issues related to submissiveness and ineffectual assertiveness (Ball, Otto, Pollack, & Rosenbaum, 1994; Petty, Sachs-Ericsson, & Joiner Jr, 2004), the intersection of primitive hostility and submissiveness in the persistently depressed individual renders their interpersonal deficits even more severe and stable over time (Constantino et al., 2008).

Persistently depressed individuals tend to experience more interpersonal distress, feel less confident that they can be assertive or aggressive when needed, while they appear to be preoccupied with avoiding humiliation and conflict with others, compared to a normative sample (Locke et al., 2015). When experiencing more difficult interpersonal life events, they tend to use avoidance or emotion-focused coping strategies that enhance negative rumination over symptoms and their causes, which have been shown to increase depressive symptoms (Enns & Cox, 2005) and are associated with poorer quality of life (Kuehner & Huffziger, 2012). Indeed, the more depressed individuals tend to have less well-rounded interpersonal patterns that are associated with more submissive and interpersonally accommodating styles of relating than the less depressed individuals (Locke et al., 2015). Furthermore, the severely depressed individuals tend to feel less confident in being able to use problem-solving strategies or avoidance strategies, such as social diversion.

These interpersonal characteristics contribute to evidence that a submissive-dependent interpersonal style is associated with greater vulnerability to depression (Bornstein, 1992; Pincus & Gurtman, 1995). Individuals with persistent depression have been described as eliciting hostile or aggressive reactions from their therapists in relation to their own passive or passive-aggressive interpersonal styles (Constantino et al., 2012; Grosse Holtforth et al., 2012; Quilty, Mainland, McBride, & Bagby, 2013). These findings support Coyne's theory that depressed individuals seek constant sympathy and attention from the environment which may become bothersome to others (Coyne, 1976). Joiner and his colleagues took Coyne's theory one step further by measuring the reassurance-seeking behaviors of depressed individuals and found these behaviors to be positively associated with depressive symptoms and with interpersonal rejection (Joiner, Alfano, & Metalsky, 1992) and pointed out the contradictory nature of the depressive's interpersonal patterns. On one hand the depressed person is observed seeking reassurance from others to enhance self-esteem but when this reassurance is obtained the authors point out that it clashes with the depressed person's negative self-image. This in turn induces doubt regarding the veracity of the validation or reassurance received, thus compelling the depressive to seek negative feedback in order to restore the negative self-concept (Hames, Hagan, & Joiner, 2013).

Thus, these patients most often perceive that the causal influences in their life are beyond their personal control. They have a poor ability to use a problem-focused coping style and problems are described in a global way, resulting in feelings of hopelessness and helplessness. These patients see their depression as going on forever and as affecting their life in a pervasive and global way, which contributes to feelings of hopelessness. They have maladaptive interpersonal styles often playing out a "victim lifestyle" when interacting with others. These patients often adopt a submissive style of interacting that makes it difficult for the therapist not to assume a more dominant role (McCullough, 2000). McCullough (2000, 2006) describes this perceptual disconnect between the depressed patient and his or her interpersonal environment, such that the depressed patient's behavior with others results in consequences that have no informing influence on the patient. He named this construct *perceived functionality* (McCullough, 2000, 2006; McCullough & Penberthy, 2011) and found it lacking in persistently depressed patients. Perceived functionality is defined as the ability to identify the consequences of one's interpersonal behavior (McCullough, Lord, Conley, & Martin, 2010) and teaching this ability is a major objective of CBASP. CBASP is a therapeutic model that targets the interpersonal-social sphere of functioning and is aimed specifically at helping persistently depressed patients learn about the stimulus value they have on others and about the impact others have on them.

CBASP HISTORY

CBASP was developed by James P. McCullough, Jr. (2000, 2006) and is the only psychotherapy system specifically designed to meet the unique needs of those suffering from persistent depression. CBASP is a highly structured, skills-oriented interpersonal approach that teaches concrete approaches to help individuals overcome interpersonal problems and reach tangible and attainable life goals. CBASP was specifically formulated to meet the challenges and clinical requirements of the persistently depressed patient. In attempting to transform habitual and treatment-resistant patterns of behavior, CBASP therapists choreograph a collaborative focus on resolving current problems of living using behavioral analytic interpersonal procedures. In CBASP, patients are perceptually connected/re-connected with the interpersonal consequences of their behavior. Once the perception of a functional connection between behavior and consequences is learned, the patient is taught the behavioral skills necessary to bring about more empathically responsive/ appropriate interactions in their specific interpersonal setting.

The emphasis in CBASP is on interpersonal social problem-solving. Interpersonal motives are at the core of these interpersonal behaviors and constitute the focus of therapeutic interventions in CBASP, while cognitions are important but only in as much as they lead to environmental-social consequences. Simultaneously, CBASP therapists deliberately manage transference issues (learned interpersonal expectancies) within the therapeutic relationship. These transference issues are manifestations of interpersonal motives that the therapist helps to identify and circumscribe. These learned expectancies, or interpersonal motives, have their roots in developmental histories of early life events of the patients. The way CBASP therapists manage and modify these transference issues and the way they understand and manage their own reactions to the patient's learned expectancies, make CBASP a unique model when compared to other treatments for depressive disorders.

The objective of this treatment manual is to present an adaptation of this successful treatment model for persistent depression to a group modality with a rationale that is explained below. This manual will provide a detailed account of the content of each group session along with the corresponding theoretical explanations. This manualized Group-CBASP treatment is more cost-effective than individual psychotherapy and will hopefully facilitate further research into its effectiveness with this population of patients as well as with other patients suffering from bipolar depression, social phobia, Post-Traumatic Stress Disorder, or other disorders co-occurring with persistent depression, such as alcohol or substance-use disorders.

CBASP RESEARCH EVIDENCE

There is a growing body of evidence from across the globe examining the effectiveness of CBASP for treating persistently depressed patients. In a multicenter randomized controlled trial in the US, Keller and his colleagues (Keller et al., 2000) compared the acute (12-week) efficacy of an antidepressant medication (nefazodone) to CBASP when administered alone and in combination with CBASP. A total of 681 patients meeting criteria for the different subtypes of chronic depression, and with a baseline Hamilton Rating Scale for Depression (HRSD-24) score of at least 20, were treated with nefazodone alone (titrated to a dose of 600 mg, $n=220$); CBASP alone (16–20 sessions, $n=216$); or a combination of both, ($n=226$). Post-therapy remission and rates of improvement (based on HRSD-24 scores) were: nefazodone (48 percent); CBASP (48 percent); combination (73 percent) (Keller et al., 2000). This study stands out as the largest and most influential study of the effects of psychotherapy versus pharmacotherapy for persistent depression, according to two meta-analyses (Cuijpers et al., 2010; von Wolff, Hölzel, Westphal, Härter, & Kriston, 2012). The effects of combined CBASP and pharmacotherapy were demonstrated to be greater than those of combined Interpersonal Psychotherapy (IPT) and pharmacotherapy (Kriston et al., 2014; von Wolff et al., 2012). The study by Keller et al. (2000) also demonstrated significantly increased effect sizes with increased number of therapy sessions, although Cuijpers et al. (2010) was the only study to demonstrate this. Results from Cuijpers et al. (2010) suggest that at least 18 sessions are needed to show optimal effects of psychotherapy. CBASP has also been identified as a possible monotherapy for the treatment of acute persistent depression, with comparable efficacy to medication (Kriston et al., 2014). A secondary analysis of the Keller et al. (2000) data suggests that psychotherapy in the form of CBASP provides additional benefit for those with a history of early adverse life events or childhood trauma (Nemeroff et al., 2003).

In a later study comparing CBASP with supportive psychotherapy as an *adjunct* to pharmacotherapy in the management of treatment-resistant chronic depression (the REVAMP Trial), Kocsis et al. (2009) failed to demonstrate a difference between the therapies, or an advantage over medication alone. The REVAMP study, however, deviated significantly from the original CBASP study design in the following ways: (1) pharmacotherapy alone was administered during the acute Phase I; (2) the non and partial responders were given an "augmented" dose of psychotherapy (CBASP or Supportive Therapy) in Phase II, after medication failed; (3) the majority of subjects opted for pharmacotherapy over psychotherapy at the outset of the study; and (4) the mean number of CBASP psychotherapy sessions was fewer than 13 (Kocsis et al., 2009). There were also some significant differences in the clinical characteristics of the patients in the two studies. These key differences may help explain the failure to replicate findings from the Keller et al. (2000) study.

In a small randomized controlled trial ($n=30$), in a German sample, a course of CBASP (mean number sessions = 21.2) was shown to have roughly equivalent efficacy to a similar course of IPT (based on clinician rated depressive symptoms). However, remission rates (mean HRSD-24) were higher for CBASP (57 percent) compared to IPT (20 percent). Eligible patients were required to have a diagnosis of early-onset depression with a baseline HRSD of ≥16 (mean 23.2) and were required to be drug free prior to and for the duration of the study. Seventy-two percent of patients (n=21) had previously experienced psychotherapy with only 21 percent (n=6) having had no prior treatment of any kind (Schramm et al., 2011). Schramm et al. nevertheless confirmed additional findings (Kriston et al., 2014) supporting the greater effectiveness of CBASP compared to IPT for early-onset persistent depression.

Swan et al. (2014) offered an open trial of CBASP to a cohort of 115 referred patients within primary and secondary care. Diagnostic interview and standardized outcome measures were administered before and after six months of CBASP with a trained, accredited therapist. Seventy-four patients entered therapy, with 46 patients completing. Thirty percent met criteria for remission (≤8 HRSD-24 score) and a further 30 percent met criteria for clinically significant change (>8 and ≤15 HRSD-24 plus 50 percent reduction in baseline score). Thirty-nine percent made "no change." Group measures of quality of life, social functioning, and interpersonal functioning also improved for these patients. Swan and colleagues determined that CBASP is an acceptable therapy for a large proportion of patients with persistent depression and that it was associated with clinically significant change in 60 percent of completers.

Wiersma et al. (2014) conducted a multisite randomized controlled trial in the Netherlands comparing CBASP and care as usual for 139 outpatients with chronic depression. Care as usual was defined as evidence-based psychotherapy such as cognitive behavioral therapy or interpersonal psychotherapy or more rarely, supportive psychotherapy. In both arms, antidepressants were provided via a guideline driven protocol with ongoing clinical management. Although the two treatment groups did not significantly differ from each other based on symptom inventories at 8, 16, and 32 weeks, they were equally comparable. Results indicate that at week 52, patients assigned to CBASP had a greater reduction of depressive symptoms compared to patients assigned to care as usual. Thus, Wiersma et al. (2014) conclude that CBASP is at least as effective as standard evidence-based treatments for chronic depression, and in the long run, CBASP appears to have an added effect.

GROUP-CBASP APPROACH

Although evidence for the treatment effectiveness of group psychotherapy for persistent depression is still limited, there is an indication that interpersonal group therapy (Schramm et al., 2008), cognitive behavioral group therapy (Bockting et al., 2005; Bristow & Bright, 1995; Matsunaga et al., 2010; Oei & Dingle, 2008; Saulsman, Coall, & Nathan, 2006; Swan et al., 2004; Teismann et al., 2013), dialectic behavior group therapy (Harley et al., 2008), and behavioral activation provided in a group setting (Dimidjian et al., 2006) are effective in significantly reducing depressive symptoms during the acute phase of the illness. Group therapy is also found to be equivalent to individual therapy in reducing depressive symptoms (Cuijpers, Van Straten, & Warmerdam, 2008; Oei & Dingle, 2008). Furthermore, there is evidence that interpersonally oriented psychotherapies are more effective for treating depression (Cuijpers, Van Straten, Andersson, & Van Oppen, 2008) compared to other therapeutic modalities.

CBASP is a predominantly interpersonal problem-solving treatment model that bases its effectiveness on whether individuals learn the consequences and impacts of their interactions both on themselves and on others by understanding their interpersonal goals and learning effective approach behavior to facilitate achievement of these goals. CBASP emphasizes this social problem-solving approach, within a motivational framework, using a manualized approach (McCullough, 2000, 2001). This model integrates principles to help increase felt emotional safety and effective interpersonal goal setting and achievement. These in turn lead to acquired learning of interpersonal perceived functionality and behavior change, which ultimately lead to improved mood and functioning. CBASP may be best learned and practiced within an interpersonal context such as that of a group. A group therapy approach provides the support needed from others experiencing similar levels of difficulties. The group provides a socializing environment where felt safety can be learned, approach behaviors encouraged, and maladaptive interpersonal interactions reviewed and revised in vivo and where new behavioral and interpersonal goals can be set and practiced within a controlled social setting. Patients may come to feel more empowered and motivated to adaptively respond to significant others in their environment and to break away from isolation and entrapment associated with persistent depression.

Patients work together toward "Desired Outcomes" (DOs) that are reasonable and attainable and learn from their own and others' reported experiences and insights. As such, the group is a social system in which learning can take place with and from others, to maximize rewards and increase pleasures that have been depleted with persistent depression. Each member is encouraged to develop a sense of belonging, acceptance, commitment, and allegiance to the group. Feelings of attachment, support, and attraction or "pulls" toward the group's efforts to resolve difficult issues together are also operating in the group's process and help articulate interpersonal goals. Finally, group members work together or separately through behavioral exchanges that can be engaging or at times distancing.

The group setting also helps to counter the individual therapist's temptation to rescue the depressed patient (McCullough, 2000) with group members instead making specific recommendations to each other on how to resolve certain difficulties. A group modality places individuals in an interactive mode in which they are repeatedly confronted with communication between group members. The group is a social network in which members can influence each other intentionally, therefore exercising personal agency and enhancing self-efficacy (Bandura, 2012).

Group members' beliefs in their capabilities develop through their experience of mastery by working together on Situational Analyses (SAs), which are challenging social problem-solving exercises. Through social modeling (Bandura, 2012), group members learn to persevere and observe how others in the group with similar depressive symptoms succeed at reaching their interpersonal goals. Finally, learning occurs through the effects of social persuasion (Bandura, 2012) with group members influencing and encouraging each other. The group also provides a naturally rewarding environment resembling the one that patients left behind or never had. The group is a form of simulation or "social laboratory" replicating to some extent reality-based, expected levels of functioning for each individual. For example, group members are expected to attend each group session or to notify of their absence in case of an emergency. Group members are also asked to respect a limited set of rules covering issues of confidentiality and acceptance to work on individual objectives. For this reason, depressed patients are often reluctant initially to participate in group therapy, which they perceive as an exposure experience to the much feared stimuli that they have successfully managed to avoid, the primary one being interactions with others. Indeed, interactions between group members can be minimal at the start of group therapy. Their interpersonal behaviors are characterized by what is described in preoperational children as "parallel play." Group members listen to others but initially they may rarely engage one another in discussion and may avoid eye contact with others in the group, especially at the beginning of group therapy. Nevertheless, the presence of other group members whom patients see as having very similar difficulties as themselves, including social avoidance, comes as a great relief to them and counteracts feelings of inadequacy and shame about their own interpersonal difficulties.

Depressed patients in a group therapy setting may openly acknowledge the difficulties they have identifying personal life goals or interpersonal goals. They may share similar experiences of dissatisfaction and frustration about feeling misunderstood by others, which in turn appear to reinforce social avoidance and the vicious cycle of defeatist thinking and hopelessness that McCullough (2000) has clearly articulated in his description of the dynamics of persistent depression. In the group setting, members work together and in parallel to understand each other's interpersonal goals or lack thereof, which is framed in terms of a "DO" obtained at the end of a specific interpersonal "slice of time," as is explained to them. They learn to solve "one problem at a time" (McCullough, 2000), in order to succeed at overcoming persistent depression.

The Situational Analysis (SA) is the main skill-acquisition exercise taught to group participants. The SA requires that participants attend to the various steps involved in the analysis of an interpersonal situation and calls on the very mentalizing executive functions that these patients are lacking and that CBASP aims to help them recover. They learn to attend to reality-based elements of an interpersonal situation such as characteristics of their nonverbal behavior within the situation outlined, the Actual *observable* Outcome of the situation as it unfolded for the patient and finally their DO for this particular situation, which needs to be under their control, realistic, and attainable. Participants are also made aware of their thoughts during the interpersonal situation described. In the revision of the SA, patients need executive cognitive functions to determine if their thoughts or "read" of the situation was relevant or not to the actual verbal exchange that took place. They learn to identify an "Action Interpretation," a self-statement, which will lead them more directly to the DO, being the interpersonal goal they previously identified. They also learn how intense emotions impede their ability to "read" an interpersonal situation accurately.

In Group-CBASP, depressed patients learn early in therapy that their interpersonal motives or goals are anything but unambiguous. These individuals often acknowledge, early on in the group, their use of avoidance strategies in the face of interpersonal conflict. They find themselves, however, in a situation of cognitive dissonance within the group, being drawn into the cohesion that develops between group members on one hand and their withdrawing behaviors in the face of this social situation on the other. Group members appear to respond to this dissonance with reticence at first and resistance to bringing difficult interpersonal situations to be discussed in the group using the SA exercise, as they are instructed to do. Their feeling is that the group is already an exposure situation that is, in many cases, more intense than what they will have experienced in a long while considering their degree of social isolation and withdrawal. Even significant others in their community appear to have accommodated to these patients' passive and helpless stance by inadvertently reinforcing maladaptive behaviors and promoting dependency when they take on a more dominant or directive role with the depressed person.

The use of Disciplined Personal Involvement (DPI), through Contingent Personal Responsivity (CPR) and the Interpersonal Discrimination Exercise (IDE), enables the CBASP therapist to "choreograph and direct the interpersonal learning processes" (McCullough et al., 2010, p. 321). The group therapist models appropriate self-disclosure behaviors aimed at underlining the consequences of the participants' maladaptive behaviors manifested within the group, such as avoidance of eye contact, late arrivals, or lack of assertiveness within the group. The IDE is used to help individuals discriminate between the fear of being rejected by others in the group and the reality-based acceptance and support received from group members.

GROUP-CBASP RESEARCH EVIDENCE

Brakemeier et al. (2011) conducted a pilot study utilizing Group-CBASP in an inpatient setting. She examined ten patients who were provided CBASP in a group setting along with pharmacotherapy and reported 100 percent completion rates of the 24 sessions over three months. Patients endorsed high satisfaction with the treatment modality. Brakemeier et al. (2011) report significant improvements and large effect sizes in both the HRSD and the Beck Depression Inventory.

In a pilot study, Sayegh et al. (2012) conducted a single arm study examining the impact of 12 sessions of Group-CBASP in 44 outpatients diagnosed with persistent depression, all of whom were also receiving pharmacotherapy managed by their psychiatrist. The findings demonstrated significant decreases in self-reported symptoms of depression and in the use of emotion-oriented coping as well as increases in overall social adjustment and interpersonal efficacy when compared to their pretreatment levels. Moreover, the effects on overall depression and social adjustment were quite strong. Sayegh et al. conducted a randomized control study examining the impact of Group-CBASP versus behavioral activation; however, results are not yet published.

Recently, Schramm et al. (2014, unpublished results) completed a randomized control trial comparing CBASP versus a mindfulness-based intervention versus treatment as usual (TAU = standard psychiatric care) to treat persistently depressed patients in a group format. Final results have not been published, but preliminary results are in prepublication and indicate that the CBASP group post-treatment HRSD and Beck Depression Inventory scores were significantly lower compared with their baseline scores, with reductions of 40.7 percent and 37.4 percent respectively. Mindfulness-Based Cognitive Therapy (MBCT) and treatment as usual (TAU) group post-treatment scores showed no statistical differences from baseline.

Group-CBASP appears to be a promising and efficient option for treating persistently depressed patients. With this Group-CBASP treatment manual, we hope to standardize the application of this therapy and thus promote additional well-controlled and much needed research and clinical care of this challenging patient population.

The Role of Medication
By James Farquhar MD, FRCPC

Antidepressant medications are an important component of a comprehensive treatment approach for persistent depression. For many patients, therapy and medication together give a better result than either medication or therapy alone. Research indicates that a combination of CBASP with antidepressant medication helps patients more than CBASP alone or medication alone (Arnow & Constantino, 2003; Keller et al., 2000), particularly for persistent depression.

The prescribing physician should monitor patients taking antidepressant medications. There are a variety of options with respect to medications and patients should be encouraged to work with their prescribing physician to find the one that works best for them. The brief summary below is intended to provide basic facts about antidepressants, but is not a substitute for patients obtaining ongoing medical care from a prescribing physician.

Since the 1990s, newer generations of antidepressants are more widely available and have fewer side effects than some of the earlier antidepressants. Commonly used antidepressants include the selective serotonin re-uptake inhibitors (SSRIs). This family includes fluoxetine (Prozac), citalopram (Celexa), escitalopram (Cipralex, Lexapro), paroxetine (Paxil), sertraline (Zoloft), and fluvoxamine (Luvox). Serotonin is a neurotransmitter used by some nerve cells in the brain to transmit electrical signals. These particular brain cells are involved in emotional circuits in the brain that regulate mood. The drugs increase the amount of serotonin available to these cells. Often, but not always, boosting the serotonin leads to improved mood and decreased depressive symptoms. This effect is fairly well established for moderate and severe depression. For mild depression, research suggests that, for many people, the drugs may be no more effective than placebo. More recently, another group of antidepressants has emerged that work in a similar way, boosting both serotonin and another mood-regulating neurotransmitter called norepinephrine. These antidepressants include venlafaxine (Effexor), desvenlafaxine (Pristiq), and duloxetine (Cymbalta). Another antidepressant, bupropion (Wellbutrin), boosts norepinephrine and dopamine.

The newer antidepressants do not necessarily work better than the old versions. On average, it appears that each antidepressant is about as effective as the others, with some individuals responding better to certain antidepressants. The primary differences between antidepressants are the side effect profiles. The positive effects of antidepressants are not seen immediately, and may take two to three weeks or more to take effect. The same delay, of two or three weeks, is observed every time the antidepressant dose is changed or if one antidepressant is stopped and another one is started. The newer antidepressants have fewer side effects, with the most common side effects being headaches and nausea. Weight gain is also sometimes seen with some antidepressants. Most commonly, weight gain can occur with paroxetine, fluvoxamine, and sertraline. Some weight loss can occur with other antidepressants including citalopram and bupropion. Additionally, some medications may increase sleep or sleepiness, and others may reduce sleep. Many patients complain of sexual side effects, including decreased libido and delayed orgasm in both males and females. The exception is bupropion, which can increase sexual interest and enhance function and pleasure.

If patients stop antidepressants abruptly they may experience withdrawal, which may include symptoms such as poor sleep, sleeping too much, flu-like symptoms, fatigue, and unpleasant changes in mood. If this happens, it is generally mild and rarely lasts more than a few days. As with any medication, it is important for the patient to observe the physician's instructions, which would usually advise tapering off the drug rather than stopping it abruptly.

Many years of research regarding antidepressants have led to official guidelines for their use by physicians. The American Psychiatric Association and the Canadian Psychiatric Association have developed the most widely used guidelines for prescribing antidepressant medications. All guidelines state clearly that drugs are only one aspect of the treatment of depression, and that psychotherapy may be the most helpful treatment, whether alone or in combination with drugs. The guidelines give suggestions about which antidepressants might be tried first, and what drug strategies may be helpful if the first medication used is not effective. These strategies include changing one antidepressant drug for another or adding an additional antidepressant or another class of drugs. The add-on treatments include lithium, thyroid hormones, and antipsychotic medications. Antipsychotics may be used as mood stabilizers or as add-on treatments for depression (Komossa et al., 2010). These drugs include quetiapine (Seroquel), olanzapine (Zyprexa), and aripiprazole (Abilify).

One risk of all antidepressants is the development of mania or hypomania, even in people who have never had these mood shifts before. Although the occurrence of such symptoms is rare, psychotherapists should be aware of the possibility. If a patient is prescribed antidepressant medications by their physician, the therapist may wish to familiarize themselves with the characteristics of the medication in order to watch for potential side effects and advise the patient to seek appropriate help if necessary.

PART

II

GROUP-CBASP METHODOLOGY AND PROCEDURE

This manual describes Group-CBASP for depressed outpatients and is designed for patients who have persistent unipolar depression as a primary diagnosis. Many of these patients will have had an early onset of their depression and many will have experienced early maltreatment or trauma. These patients are hypothesized to have learned fear that leads to avoidance of others and social isolation. They demonstrate interpersonal withdrawal and derailment and/or arrest of normal cognitive-emotional maturational growth with subsequent negative consequences in social functioning (Inoue, Tonooka, Yamada, & Kanba, 2004; Inoue, Yamada, & Kanba, 2006; McCullough, 2000, 2006; Schnell, Bluschke, Konradt, & Walter, 2011), which lead to worsening depressive symptoms. In the CBASP model, this interpersonal fear/avoidance is proposed as the core psychopathology of the persistently depressed individual, thus Group-CBASP therapists must be willing and able to work with avoidant, hostile/detached patients. The nature of the patient's difficulties underscores the critical role of the group therapist in promoting the supportive and reinforcing aspects of strong group cohesion and in using the group setting as a socializing environment to help depressed individuals understand the impact of their predominantly passive, unassertive, and non-dominant behaviors on others in their environment.

It is advised that the patient's diagnosis be made prior to starting Group-CBASP and that required pharmacotherapy is initiated prior to or at the time of group initiation. The Group-CBASP therapist meets with each potential group participant individually for at least one or two sessions prior to the beginning of the group to carry out a diagnostic assessment as well as a structured developmental history called the Significant Other History (SOH), which is used to determine and define the patient's interpersonal learning history. Information from this interpersonal history provides a valuable understanding of the patient and also informs the therapist's role. Additionally, the depression time-line exercise (**Handout 1 in Workbook**) is used to help patients visualize the evolution of their depressive episodes over time and chart their levels of severity, associated life events, and impact of depressive symptoms on their overall functioning.

All references made in this manual to Handouts refer to forms that are available to distribute to patients and that are found in the patient's workbook, not in this manual, to avoid duplication. Only a limited number of Handouts

are reproduced in the therapist's manual to help explain concepts. For that reason, the numbering of the Handouts will refer to the sequence found in the patient's workbook.

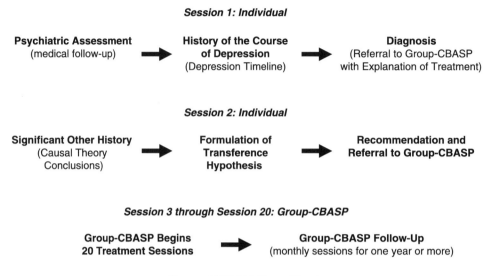

Group-CBASP Flow Chart

SELECTION CRITERIA

Patients diagnosed with a major or persistent depression, who agree to participate in the group and who have completed the preparatory exercises, are provided with information regarding the structure of the group. Therapists and clinics may vary in their choice of certain aspects of the group's structure, such as the number of patients to include; the duration of each session (90 to 120 minutes); bi-weekly sessions at the beginning and weekly sessions toward the end with monthly sessions for follow-up; and the total number of group sessions provided (from 20 to 24 or more), however the current authors use the following guidelines:

- A maximum of six or seven patients per group.
- Group sessions of two-hour duration provided weekly.
- Twenty consecutive weeks of group sessions (this number of sessions is supported by research evidence for the need to extend sessions beyond the initial 12 weeks used in the multisite research study of Keller at al., 2000).
- Follow-up monthly group sessions (optional but helpful) to maintain learning and prevent relapse.

The current authors have favored the decision to constitute groups that are homogeneous with regards to level of functioning and with regards to primary diagnosis of persistent depression. As for individuals with personality disorders, it is up to each therapist to use his or her clinical judgment to determine whether an individual is able or not to benefit from a group setting at the time of the assessment.

Not all patients will be suitable for Group-CBASP. Group-CBASP is designed and tested for people with persistent depression and may be used with people who have trauma histories, including abuse and neglect. It is not recommended for patients with severe psychomotor impairment, which prevents them from functioning in a group setting, or for chronically suicidal or antisocial patients, as these patients need individualized intervention tailored to their particular difficulties and needs. Group-CBASP is not recommended for patients actively abusing substances. However, these patients may initiate participation in a substance-abuse program concurrently as they attend Group-CBASP and must be abstinent during group sessions. Patients with active psychotic symptoms may find the group setting very anxiety provoking, and are not suitable for Group-CBASP. Group-CBASP may be adapted to help certain patients with psychotic depression learn to ground themselves in the behavioral and reality-based anchors of an interpersonal situation. A discussion of how to accurately describe the Actual Outcome (AO) according to observable and behavioral indicators, for example, can help such a patient discriminate between ideas of reference or delusional thinking and the reality-based outcome of the interpersonal slice of time. Patients in a hypomanic phase of a bipolar disorder may experience difficulties cooperating with others to solve interpersonal problems due to higher irritability or to racing thoughts and may need to focus on more primary concerns such as medication adjustments, disturbed sleep, irritability, agitation, and other manic or hypomanic symptoms and behaviors.

TRAINING FOR CLINICIANS

CBASP is a sophisticated interpersonal problem-solving psychotherapy system that involves a unique personal Disciplined Involvement of the therapist/clinician. One of the major goals of CBASP psychotherapy is to teach this patient to interact interpersonally in more effective ways, which necessitates that patients learn to generate empathy with the therapist and others. This kind of reciprocal interpersonal functioning is characterized as a criterion for wellness in CBASP and each of the therapeutic techniques of CBASP is designed to teach interpersonal problem-solving behavior. As such, the role of the clinician in administering CBASP and Group-CBASP is pivotal. The group leader must foster felt emotional safety for the group members in order to promote learning, while simultaneously orchestrating the CBASP techniques to increase approach behaviors and effective interpersonal functioning and increased perceived abilities to achieve realistic and attainable goals set by the patient. This is no small feat and requires a skilled, knowledgeable, and mature clinician who is well aware of his or her own interpersonal impact and vulnerabilities. Thus, CBASP and Group-CBASP are designed to be implemented by licensed trained mental health care professionals such as clinical or counselling psychologists, psychiatrists, psychiatric nurse practitioners, or clinical social workers with at least two years of experience with this patient population and who have completed specific CBASP training.

Specific training in CBASP is required prior to implementing Group-CBASP, and additional training in Group-CBASP is recommended. Training in CBASP and Group-CBASP can be obtained via the CBASP Training Institute or the CBASP Network and information regarding these organizations can be found online at www.cbasp.org/, www.cbaspsociety.org/, and www.cbasp-network.org/. Certification in CBASP and/or Group-CBASP is available and the specifics of training may vary from country to country. Specific standards exist in the US and Canada as well as in the UK, Germany, Switzerland, Finland, and the Netherlands. This patient population has a high risk for suicidality and co-morbidities and the implementation of CBASP and Group-CBASP should be approached with care and preparation. Significant training in CBASP, preferably with ongoing supervision, is required to most effectively administer this treatment approach while maintaining the safety of persistently depressed patients.

CBASP therapists who achieve success with the persistently depressed adult possess abilities to:

- commit to learning the CBASP and Group-CBASP methodology;
- allow the patient to "set the pace" of the therapy session;
- let the patient do the work of change; yet,
- exert structural control of the therapy session;
- tolerate in-session anxiety without needing to reflexively reduce the anxiety by changing the subject or redirecting the patient's attention to another subject;
- accept supervision and be informed by supervisory feedback;
- focus the patient's attention on the therapist himself/herself; and
- be personally vulnerable in interactions with the patient.

THE SIGNIFICANT OTHER HISTORY (SOH) EXERCISE AND TRANSFERENCE HYPOTHESIS (TH)

Following the establishment of the psychiatric diagnosis with a patient and an exploration of the course of depressive episodes, the patient who meets inclusion criteria for Group-CBASP is invited to attend one or two individual sessions to discuss the benefits of Group-CBASP for him or her. These meetings take place prior to enrolment into Group-CBASP. The group therapist explains how the treatment model works and the benefits of Group-CBASP as an interpersonal problem-solving approach to enhance social functioning and reduce depressive symptoms. This assessment allows the therapist to determine whether the patient is a good candidate for Group-CBASP and to initiate an exercise called the Significant Other History (SOH) (**Form 3 in Appendix**) that will lead to the development of the Transference Hypothesis (TH), a necessary step for CBASP treatments whether in individual or group therapy. This exercise has been very well documented and is described in detail elsewhere (McCullough, 2000; McCullough et al., 2011; McCullough & Penberthy, 2011).

The SOH is an emotional interpersonal history procedure which facilitates elicitation of explicit earlier informing experiences that the depressed individual had with significant others. These prior experiences are conceptualized as learned social-emotional expectancies that inform the patient's interactions and are hypothesized to be transferred onto the clinician and other group members. These expectancies often involve themes of fear and avoidance and are grouped into four primary domains or categories. These four "transference domains of interaction" (McCullough, 2000, p. 90) include:

1. Moments in which *interpersonal intimacy* is felt/verbalized by either the group member or by the therapist.
2. Situations in which the group member *discloses/expresses emotional needs* to others in the group either directly or indirectly.
3. Situations in which a group member *fails at something* or *makes an obvious mistake* during a group session (such as learning the SA).
4. Situations in which *negative affect* (fear, frustration, anger, etc.) is obviously felt or expressed, either directly or indirectly, by a group member either toward others in the group or perhaps toward a person outside the group.

The elicitation of the SOH is led by the clinician in a semi-structured fashion and generally is comprised of three questions asked to the patient (**Form 3 in Appendix**) in order to determine how the patient's significant others have contributed, in a positive or negative way, to whom the patient has become today.

The patient is typically asked:

Step 1: "Please name three to five significant individuals in your life who have contributed in a positive or negative way to making you the person you are today."

Step 2: The therapist writes on a board or on a sheet the name of each significant other, and then begins with the first person listed and follows with the others in the order they were given by the patient, asking the patient:

Step 3:

- "Let's begin with your 'mother' (for example). What was it like growing up with your mother?"

The patient goes on to briefly describe his or her relationship with the mother while the therapist encourages the patient to speak about the effects of the mother's behavior on him or her and then asks:

- "How has your mother influenced the course of your life?"

The patient then is encouraged to describe his or her own perception of the mother's influence regardless of any cognitive distortion that this may reveal. The therapist records the patient's own words or may sometimes have to prompt the patient with some suggestions. The therapist then asks:

Step 4:

- "How has this relationship with your mother contributed to making you the person you are today?" or
- "What effect has your mother's behavior had upon the way you live?"

According to McCullough,

> the goal of this last step (this is a Piagetian mismatching exercise) is to have the patient formulate one *Causal Theory Conclusion* for each Significant Other. The *Conclusion* should represent the "stamp" or "legacy" that the patient feels the Significant Other has left on him or her that influenced the patient to be whom he or she is NOW, RIGHT NOW, TODAY!
>
> (McCullough, 2008, p. 28)

The purpose of the exercise is to help the patient initiate an "antecedent/consequence" connection between past interactions with these significant others and the patient's current functioning. McCullough cautions therapists to avoid an open-ended discussion about the patient's past, focusing instead on "consequence phrases," that is, conclusions about the impact of significant others on their life. As McCullough (2000) describes, patients may be surprised at the outcome of this exercise and many will reveal that they had never thought about the impact of significant others on their life. This initiates within patients causal inferences about interactions between themselves and others that are later linked to the outcomes they obtain in their interpersonal interactions with others and to their feelings of loss of control over these outcomes. Based upon the answers to the SOH questions, a "causal theory conclusion" or "stamp" (as McCullough calls it) is obtained for each significant other the patient has named. The patient also completes the CBASP Interpersonal Questionnaire (**Forms 4 &**

5 in Appendix) aimed at helping identify a self-rated area of interpersonal difficulty that contributes to the clinician's formulation of the TH, which itself may not have yet come to the patient's awareness.

These causal theory conclusions, as well as the result on the Interpersonal Questionnaire, are examined and used to formulate only one single TH which identifies one of the four interpersonal domains that represents a "core content of each patient's interpersonal fear" (McCullough et al., 2010, p. 324). The TH is based on the causal inferences, "stamps," or impacts that significant others have had on the patient and is formulated in an "if . . ., then . . ." statement, such as "if I express a negative emotion within the group, then the group members will reject me." A complete example of a fictitious case (Alice, **Form 6**) is described in the Appendix along with the stamps from the SOH, results of the Interpersonal Questionnaire, the formulated TH, and information on the case described later in this manual.

McCullough (2000) explains that these four transference domains of interaction were chosen to reflect the "maltreatment themes" that chronically depressed patients typically report, such as getting close to a significant other, experiencing emotional needs with a significant other, failing or making mistakes around a significant other, and having negative feelings toward a significant other. The "If this . . . then that" interpersonal hypotheses held by depressed patients comes to represent knowledge that is not within their field of awareness, since the characteristic global thinking of chronically depressed individuals may preclude the ability to think about the connections between their behaviors and the consequences they experience. McCullough et al. (2011) recommend that the TH may be modified later during therapy if it does not adequately describe the patient's core interpersonal fear or difficulty. Only one TH per patient is constructed to encourage the working through of at least one area of interpersonal difficulty throughout group therapy. The reader is encouraged to consult McCullough's descriptive publications documenting the procedure used to conduct the SOH and formulate the TH. Collaboratively arriving at the TH for the patient is a process that contributes to building the therapeutic alliance and may provide insight into the patient's awareness of current interpersonal difficulties. The TH also helps chronically depressed patients understand the link between depression and its impact on interpersonal goals and functioning. The benefits of working within a group modality become clearer to patients as they begin to think of their problems within an interpersonal approach. After the TH has been formulated, the therapist can then enlist the patient's informed consent to work within a group modality.

Each group member begins Group-CBASP having formulated a TH with the therapist in an: *if (one of the four domains is manifested in the group) . . . then (group members may respond in an anticipated negative way) format*. The TH will be integrated within the group work from the start and serves as a measure of acquisition learning. This learning is the basis upon which participants begin to discriminate between the safety experienced within the group and the malevolent significant others who have hurt them or with whom there has been a deficit in early attachment (Shaver & Mikulincer, 2011). Participants discuss their TH with others within the group and it becomes the central motive or objective for their group work. Some group members will have been able to clearly identify and understand at the initial individual interview the importance of the Interpersonal Domain as being the one they want to work on and improve during group therapy. These individuals are more aware of having learned maladaptive coping behaviors and strategies but do not yet see the impact of these on others nor do they take responsibility for the consequences of these behaviors. It is possible with these individuals to formulate a sentence that modifies one behavior in the TH and orients the person toward change. Other individuals who are less clear about what they want or need to change with regards to interpersonal motives, or who have little insight into causal inferences between themselves and others, often learn from others during group therapy and gain a better understanding of how their Interpersonal Domain manifests itself within the group. Varying levels of awareness and insight within the group can stimulate learning and contribute to group cohesion.

At the beginning of group therapy it is often very difficult for group members to discuss the way that these interpersonal domains are problematic in their lives, as these learned expectancies are often at the heart of their avoidance behaviors. Persistently depressed individuals may also develop strategies to protect themselves from the negative outcomes outlined in their respective TH. For example, an individual may avoid disclosing needs and feelings to others because he/she expects the hurtful humiliation experienced from malevolent significant others in the past. Instead, this person may please others in order to avoid anticipated reprimand or in the hope of gaining the long-awaited love and recognition from others. In time, this strategy of pleasing others comes to replace the need for self-disclosure, albeit unconsciously, and it becomes so demanding to constantly please others that the individual may choose to avoid others altogether in order to minimize the increasing burden of trying to please them. Although an individual may agree that the Interpersonal Domain of disclosing needs or feelings to others is problematic for him/her, it may not be obvious to this person that he/she developed the strategy of pleasing others to protect the self from a perceived negative outcome associated with self-disclosure. The link between the Interpersonal Domain, which needs to be the salient motive (Horowitz et al., 2006) that individuals want to work on in therapy, and the maladaptive strategies developed to cope while trying to resolve problems associated with this most salient motive, can be made more explicit in group therapy. The Group-CBASP therapist and group members all work together toward adaptive, realistic, and attainable DOs that are grounded in specific interpersonal situations while these specific situations in turn often shed light on the particular social domain of difficulty that each person gradually comes to understand.

Group members may not understand at the beginning of group therapy how their TH will be worked through within the group setting. They are often unaware of the coping strategies they have acquired because of their social-emotional learning history. During group therapy, members often begin to see their own behavioral strategies used defensively in their interactions with other group members or used to avoid rejection or embarrassment, or to gain attention, even though they increasingly feel safe and engaged within the group.

The Group-CBASP therapist uses Disciplined Involvement strategies (described below) to demonstrate the consequences of participants' maladaptive or defensive behaviors by discussing their impact on himself/herself or on others. The therapist also reinforces group members' adaptive reactions to each other's maladaptive or defensive behaviors. These in vivo consequences to group members' defensive behaviors place group members in a "mismatching" experience. This mobilizes formal operations thinking or mentalizing functions of the depressed person to understand and respond to the discrepancy between felt safety acquired within the group and their own maladaptive behaviors that have not yet been extinguished. Group members most often resolve this mismatch by choosing to change their maladaptive behaviors at least within the group. Gradually, these maladaptive strategies are replaced with more "approach" risk-taking behaviors within the group, and involve the unique interpersonal domains identified by each member as the central important motive to work on in group therapy. That is, the group members begin to disclose their feelings, acknowledge errors, let others get close, and express frustrations more easily. This learning also generalizes, and group members often report, similar approaches or risk-taking behaviors outside group therapy sessions with significant others in their lives.

The IDE can be used to help group members see the impact of their behaviors on others in the group when they attempt, consciously or not, to manifest a behavior related to their established Interpersonal Domain. More interactive exchanges take place within the group as the group therapist keeps the focus on working with SAs. Group members can see the value of a DO, in an interpersonal "slice of time," as helping them gain control over the impact they can and come to want to have on others, just as they have learned of the impact that they have on members within the group. The concept of "solving one problem at a time" becomes clearer as group members see the gains they make with each new SA.

THE SITUATIONAL ANALYSIS (SA) (COPING SURVEY QUESTIONNAIRE) WITHIN A GROUP SETTING

The therapist introduces the SA exercise as an interpersonal problem-solving strategy that can ultimately help break the vicious cycle of hopelessness and powerlessness in persistent depression. This exercise is described in great detail by McCullough (2000) who provides the rationale and objectives for each step of the exercise. The SA is described in this workbook in the form adapted to a group modality. Although the same rationale and objectives described by McCullough apply to the group application, the empowering effects of group learning and sharing are hypothesized to expand exposure and enhance the experience for participants. Patients are encouraged to regain control over their lives by solving one interpersonal problem at a time.

Each group member is encouraged to present a recent stressful or emotional interpersonal interaction that they have recently experienced. The group member explains the context in which the exchange took place and the therapist first teaches members how to choose a particular *"slice of time"* from the exchange. This period of time must have a clear beginning, middle, and an end, each marked by distinguishable behaviors. The therapist explains that the entire SA exercise will be centered on this specific *"slice of time."* This helps maintain the focus on the link between each step of the problem-solving strategy and the corresponding outcome or consequence. An example is given of a telephone call or movie clip, which begins and ends with a specific marking point and contains behaviors and statements in the middle.

The SA exercise is sometimes challenging for group members to learn as it engages the mentalizing and executive functions that are found to be lacking or diminished in patients with persistent depression. For this reason, two to three sessions are dedicated to explaining the SA using an example provided by each group member in turn. The tendency may be for group members to deny having interpersonal problems as they often report preferring to avoid conflict and withdrawing from almost all social interactions. Discussions about weekly challenges or behavioral activation steps often reveal social interactions group members had but don't consider important to mention as possible SAs. The therapist can suggest these situations as a good place to start. The SA exercise is divided into the elicitation and remediation phases and reviewed together as a group. Specifics of how to conduct the elicitation and remediation phases of SA are described in Part III of this manual.

DISCIPLINED PERSONAL INVOLVEMENT (DPI)

CBASP therapists use DPI with persistently depressed patients as a form of *therapist role enactment* based on principles of learning theory. DPI is used within two distinct therapeutic strategies in CBASP, namely the IDE and CPR. In these strategies, the therapist sets up personal response contingencies within the session to help patients immediately see the consequences of their own behaviors on themselves and on others and also to heal trauma experiences endured within abusive, invalidating, or neglectful relationships. To do this, the therapist models appropriate authentic involvement with the patient while always maintaining a therapeutic stance in which the therapist's personal needs do not factor into the equation. In addition, McCullough specifies that personal involvement does not mean that the usual boundaries of the therapeutic relationship are overthrown or violated. The therapist can nevertheless become a "comrade" (McCullough, 2006, p. 47) to the patient interacting on a reciprocal person-to-person basis, in contrast to the way negative significant others have done in the patient's life. McCullough also forewarns therapists of the importance of gaining a good understanding of the persistently depressed adult and of his or her psychopathology and its interpersonal consequences in order to establish a useful treatment plan. Among the many recommendations, McCullough cautions therapists to avoid overestimating the capabilities of the depressed patient and also to avoid doing the work of therapy for the patient. This is particularly important with the use of Disciplined Involvement as the therapist may overwhelm the patient with a personal response that does not resonate empathically with the patient's current cognitive-emotional state.

CBASP adopts an interactive approach to working with depressed patients where the rigid interpersonal behavior of the patient elicits contingent personal reactions or responses from the therapist and from others in the group. These reactions or responses are underlined and reinforced by the therapist who plays an active role in shaping the patients' behaviors toward attainable goals. From a position of perceptual disengagement, resulting from social isolation, the patient experiences the therapist's and group members' personal engagement and learns to respond in kind. The patient experiences the consequences of his or her behaviors, adaptive or maladaptive, through their impact on the therapist and group members who react appropriately yet authentically. The patient most often chooses to modify maladaptive behaviors as he or she overcomes the interpersonal fear and joins the therapist and group members in a safe and constructive therapeutic alliance expressed through the group's cohesion. Interpersonal avoidance or emotion-focused coping are gradually replaced by interpersonal reciprocity and personal involvement between group members which lead the depressed patient to develop greater self-efficacy and improved social functioning (Sayegh et al., 2012). Patients acquire *perceived functionality* when they learn that their behaviors can have consequences on others.

CBASP helps depressed patients move . . .

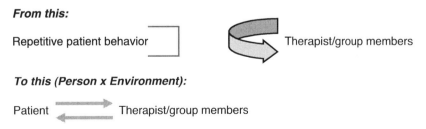

This is recognition of interpersonal consequences of one's behavior (perceived functionality).

THE INTERPERSONAL DISCRIMINATION EXERCISE (IDE)

The IDE, requiring DPI on the part of therapist, is one of the core components of individual and Group-CBASP. It is used whenever the patient, in individual or group therapy, enacts a behavior related to the TH of the Interpersonal Domain (intimacy, disclosure, mistakes/errors, or expressed negative emotions) that has been identified as being a "hot spot" for this particular patient. The therapist or any group member expresses their response to the patient, regarding this "hot spot," in such a way that is usually contrary to the punitive or negative response this patient would have received from a malevolent significant other. This healing experience involves a negative reinforcement condition in which the aversive situation (being criticized by the malevolent significant other) is replaced by the facilitative response of the therapist or group members in a reassuring and nonthreatening way. The positive interpersonal experience is reinforced by the therapist who draws attention to the distinction between the patient's experience with hurtful significant others and the current supportive responses from the group.

A suggested strategy for using the IDE in Group-CBASP is to ask each group member, at the beginning of each session, to choose one card on which the TH of one of the group members is written and to pay attention throughout the session to whether the person named on the card expressed any behavior or comments related in any way to their TH. This works quite well in our experience since group members find it easier to pay attention to each other's TH than to their own. The therapist also models appropriate personal involvement with all group members and adopts an active stance to encourage participants to give each other feedback regarding their THs. The therapist keeps the focus on discriminating between past learning and current reactions within the group.

An example of an IDE in Group-CBASP:

- A group member did not attend one of the group sessions and did not call to notify the clinic about his absence, as is requested. The group wondered where he was and some reacted with surprise that he had not called. This patient came to the following group session and did not make any mention of his absence the previous week, nor did any other participant ask him why he had not come. After waiting to see if he would explain his absence, the therapist did ask where he was the previous week. The patient mentioned, in a dismissive tone, that he had not been able to attend and forgot to call. The therapist asked for more detail about his absence and for more information about his forgetting to call to which the patient appeared annoyed and repeated that he had not thought to call and proceeded to apologize. The therapist turned to the group to inquire about others' perceptions regarding this patient's absence and the fact that he did not call. After a brief silence from the group, one member expressed concern for him considering a personal disclosure the patient had shared with the group the week prior to his absence about feeling more down and pessimistic about his unsuccessful job search. The patient was surprised to see that his absence had an impact on others. After some discussion of the impact of his absence on group members, the patient responded with surprise that his absence did not go unnoticed which implied that his presence matters because he is important to the functioning of the group.
- This patient's TH was related to the domain of making mistakes and consequently fearing that others might find him "inadequate" or "ridiculous."
- Following some discussion within the group recalling the patient's TH and its relevance in this situation, the therapist asked the patient to reflect on a comparison between a reaction his father would have had and the group's reaction this week to his unannounced absence the previous week:

- "How would your father have responded to you if you had not shown up for an activity that you both had planned and had forgotten to call him?" The patient explained that his father is unforgiving and would dismiss him as being inadequate. The therapist then asked the patient "How did we in the group respond to you forgetting to call?" The patient replied feeling surprised that his presence matters to the group and that others are concerned about his wellbeing. His initial reaction was one of guilt about doing the "wrong thing," that is not calling the therapist, but it took some time for this patient to realize that the issue was more about the group's concern for his safety and the realization that he is an important member of the group, rather than focusing on criticism of his behavior. He confirmed that it had not occurred to him that his presence or absence would have an impact on others in the group as this was related to him feeling unimportant. This patient was aware of self-sabotaging behaviors and had come to expect criticism or punishment rather than concern. The group members' engaging behaviors during the IDE contrasted with the patient's behaviors that appear to push others away (by not attending the session and not calling). The patient realized that his behaviors did not agree with his values as he does not want to push others away, particularly not the participants in the group to whom he felt much closer. This experience marked a turning point in this patient's trajectory toward recovery on which he continued to build and learn. He eventually shed many of his maladaptive behaviors that were inadvertently pushing others away as he himself identified that he was not behaving as a "responsible adult."

The IDE is completed when the therapist has drawn the patient's attention to new learning acquired by him or her through this exercise and by discussing within the group what each member can learn from the particular example. In addition, the therapist underlines the discrepancy between the reaction of punitive significant others and those of the therapist or group members in this situation, otherwise patients will often overlook the positive reactions gained from feeling safe with others. New learning is reinforced as old learning is extinguished.

CONTINGENT PERSONAL RESPONSIVITY (CPR)

The CBASP therapist also uses DPI in "contingent, unilateral ways to inform the interpersonal behavior of patients and to break through the preoperational barriers that inhibit bidirectional behavior" (McCullough, 2006, p. 58). This means that the therapist remains actively engaged within the group throughout treatment in such a way as to demonstrate to group members that what they say and do within the group has an impact on others. The therapist uses the strategy of CPR, another core component of CBASP, to respond to group members in such a way as to help modify their maladaptive interpersonal behaviors. To do this, the therapist must first become aware of his or her interpersonal reaction toward each group member; that is, each group member's stimulus value to the therapist. This is achieved by the therapist completing the Impact Message Inventory (IMI) (described in sessions 9 and 10 under The Interpersonal Circumplex in Group-CBASP in Part III) and then plotting the results on the Interpersonal Circumplex, indicating the therapist's reaction to each group member. Please refer to sessions 13 and 14 in Part III for further elaboration of the use of CPR in a group setting. We will limit the discussion of CPR here by saying that the group therapist models a friendly or friendly–dominant role by remaining actively engaged and responding in an authentic but disciplined way whenever the TH has been activated for any group member.

GROUP-CBASP SESSIONS OUTLINE

Part III outlines material covered in each group session. These outlines are meant as a guide and can easily be adapted to the varying needs of a particular patient population. Participants assimilate the information at different rates and groups vary in their dynamics and in the overall level of functioning of their members. It is up to the clinical judgment of the group therapist to determine if more time is needed to learn the SA. Additionally, the Interpersonal Circumplex may be too complex for some groups whose members may be less psychologically minded. It is important that the group therapist allows group members to set the pace at which they need to work and not the other way around. Patients with chronic depression will quickly withdraw emotionally and may drop out of the group if they feel pressured to perform or if they cannot find a way to make the group useful for them. The Group-CBASP strategies are always at the service of the therapy to help individuals recover from depression.

It is important to remember that the **core components** of Group-CBASP include:

1. The SOH and generation of the TH.
2. The SA exercise with elicitation and remediation phases.
3. Disciplined Involvement using the IDE and CPR.

The Interpersonal Circumplex described later on in the manual is used as a psycho-educational tool to help explain some principles of interpersonal behaviors but is **not an essential component of CBASP**. Some therapists may decide to leave this section out and focus only on using SAs along with an engaged, active DPI with group members. In fact, some more highly functioning groups may not need any prompting with psycho-education to convince them of the benefits of understanding their impact on others.

PART

GROUP-CBASP SESSIONS

GROUP-CBASP SESSIONS 1–20

This section of the manual describes the content of group sessions from beginning to end. We recommend that therapists follow the progression of material as it is presented in the first six to seven sessions. The first session introduces members to each other and includes a discussion of the difficulties patients have experienced with depression, medication, and the cost of depression in various aspects of their lives. The second session includes a discussion of the lifestyle of each group member, with particular attention paid to necessary changes needed to improve overall quality of life, including pleasurable and rewarding activities that are gradually reintroduced using the concept of graded tasks. These two sessions provide the groundwork to introduce the CBASP model in the third session in which loss of control over one's life is presented as being a result of global thinking and maladaptive coping strategies such as social avoidance and withdrawal. The outcome of avoidance is a feeling of hopelessness and helplessness. The therapist introduces the concept of "solving one problem at a time" using the SA. The impact of patients' behaviors on others and whether these behaviors need to be modified in order to reach the goals that patients set for themselves is presented and discussed in a broad fashion in these early sessions.

Sessions 4 to 7 are spent learning the steps of the SA and practicing them within the group with each group member taking a turn presenting a problematic interpersonal situation to be discussed. Therapists may decide to spend the rest of the 20 sessions doing SAs along with a discussion of the impact of the TH on interactions within the group. Some higher functioning groups do not need much prompting to discuss their interpersonal difficulties, particularly when they feel accepted and supported by other group members who share and understand their experiences. These groups may not need to use the Interpersonal Circumplex presented in sessions 9 to 14, although they may be interested in discussing their interpersonal dispositions or interpersonal style depicted on the circumplex using measures that are suggested and discussed in later sessions.

Using psycho-educational material, as described in sessions 9 to 14, to explain the importance of reciprocal interactions and of our motives to interact with one another is very helpful for therapists when the level of passive hostility and low motivation for change are high within lower functioning groups. These groups may contain members who have very limited interactions during the week and whose contacts with other group members may be the only ones they have due to their social isolation. Introducing these withdrawn group members to basic information about why we interact with each other, about what complementary interactions are, and showing them their own interpersonal styles depicted on the Interpersonal Circumplex generates a dynamic discussion that never fails to capture their attention and curiosity. The therapist uses the concepts described in these sessions on the Interpersonal Circumplex with the sole purpose of demonstrating more visually how submissive, overly accommodating, and avoidant behaviors help explain their difficulties in getting what they want from others. The more passive patients often have not thought about whether their maladaptive coping strategies are responsible for the dissatisfaction they feel in interactions with others. All patients want to feel more in control of their lives and all have come to feel that social isolation maintains their depressed mood. The psycho-educational material enables these more passive patients to understand the usefulness of knowing what you want in an interaction with another person and they see the consequence of not knowing.

The sessions outlined in Part III include the necessary core concepts of the CBASP model in the first half and additional sessions in the second half to support the continued practice of SA with the help of some psycho-education on the usefulness of these SAs. Therapists will use their clinical skills and judgment to adapt the material to the particular needs of the group including their level of understanding and level of functioning. To do this, the therapist needs to follow the pace of the group members and allow them to take ownership of the group and steer it in the direction that is helpful to them.

GROUP-CBASP: SESSION 1

Session outline:

- Presentation of group members
- Group-CBASP therapy sessions outline
- Group agreements
- Assessing your current depressive symptoms
- Persistent versus major depression?
- Do you have Major Depressive Disorder?
- Do you have Persistent Depressive Disorder (Dysthymia)?
- Course profiles for Persistent Depressive Disorders
- Two types of persistent depression
- What has been the course of your depression?
- Depression Timeline Worksheet
- What has been the cost of your depression?
- The Mood Chart
- General Guidelines about medication for depression
- Homework: Activity Log

We will begin today with an informal discussion about depression, the symptoms you experience now, the ways that you cope and the course that your depression has taken from the beginning to the present. We will look at various ways that each one of you may have arrived at a diagnosis of persistent depression or perhaps of major depression. We will discuss medication and we may decide to invite a nurse clinician to answer some of your questions about various medications and their side effects. We will also answer any questions you may have about what we will be doing together for the following 20 weeks of group therapy.

Welcome!

Homework: For next week, please fill out the Activity Log (see **Handout 4** in Workbook) showing how you typically spend your time during one entire week. Include meals, getting up, showering, naps, and even short walks. Include of course any social contacts and activities. Also, monitor your mood with the Mood Chart.

PRESENTATIONS, ROLES OF GROUP MEMBERS AND GROUP LEADER

During the very first group session, group members begin with brief personal introductions followed by a presentation by the group therapist of the outline of all group sessions (see in workbook: CBASP Group Therapy for Depression: Sessions Outline). Some basic group rules, preferably called Group Agreements (see patient's workbook for a copy of the agreements), are discussed and questions about procedures are answered and apprehensions about being in a group are heard. The Group-CBASP therapist assumes a directive role for this part of group discussions and informs the group of the focus and attention he or she will place on interactions among all group members throughout group therapy. The following roles of group members and of the therapist can be discussed to help clarify expectations and introduce the interpersonal approach used in CBASP. These roles are in the introductory part of the patient's workbook, before session 1, to encourage a focus on more personal introductions within the first session in a more relaxed atmosphere.

Group Members' Role

The responsibilities that each group member accepts include:

1. Agreeing to work in an interpersonal context within the group where feedback is shared respectfully.
2. Engaging in self-reflection regarding the nature of interpersonal experiences within or outside the group.
3. Completing homework assignments to improve learning.
4. Increasing activity levels using graded tasks.
5. Maintaining motivation toward change.

Group Leader's Role

The responsibilities of the group therapist leader include:

1. Facilitating group members' interactions, and the impact and consequences of such expression.
2. Adopting an active style of leadership, helping group members to work toward their goals.
3. Responding to individual group members in an open and honest way to promote growth, discuss behavioral consequences, and address conflict.
4. Attending to the stages of the group's development in order to foster a healthy, safe, and trusting group environment.

DEPRESSION

Following a brief discussion about expectations and roles, the therapist may distribute a copy of any self-report assessment of depressive symptoms, such as the Inventory of Depressive Symptoms-Self-Report (IDS-SR, Trivedi et al., 2004) or its shorter version the Quick IDS, found for free at the following website (www. ids-qids.org/). Group members complete the form given to them, regarding their symptoms over the past week, then a discussion about each person's total score and individual symptoms is held. This helps the new and often uncomfortable members talk about their depressive symptoms while maintaining some degree of privacy regarding other personal issues they would rather not reveal at the present time. Discussion follows on the particular manifestations of depressive symptoms for each member and an indication of the level of severity of their symptoms determined by the total score obtained on the questionnaire.

Following this first group discussion, the group therapist reviews the diagnostic criteria for a Major Depressive Disorder (**Form 1 in Appendix**) and discusses how this differs from dysthymia. The same is done with criteria for Persistent Depressive Disorder (**Form 2 in Appendix**). The group leader uses graphs to describe the various profiles of persistent depression, allowing members to get a better understanding of the manifestations of their illness. Definitions of relapse and recurrence are also discussed and the importance of compliance and maintenance of treatment is reinforced.

COST OF DEPRESSION

Another group discussion is held concerning the particular course of each member's depressive symptoms and illness. The leader initiates a group discussion regarding the impact of depression in the members' lives. Members may be reassured to hear that others share similar experiences regarding the "cost" of depression in various aspects of their lives (physical, professional, social, personal, and psychological), which helps them feel that they are not "alone in the world." This step also allows the leader to better understand the role of depression in the lives of the members and serves as a method to heighten the awareness and motivation of the participants regarding the negative impact of their depression and their desire to improve. The Depression Timeline Worksheet (McCullough, 2001) (**Handout 1 in Workbook**) is used to track changes in severity of depressive symptoms over time and identify events that help recall mood changes.

A discussion about medication is very helpful to group members, particularly when a nurse clinician can attend to answer questions and describe some modes of action of different medications as well as side effects. The degree of information provided may vary from one group to another and according to resources available.

CHARTING MOOD

This first group session ends with a request that group members should chart their mood over the course of the next month using a Mood Chart (**Handout 2 in Appendix**) provided. Homework for the following week consists in group members charting on an Activity Log (**Handout 4 in Workbook**) their typical activities of the next week including times at which they wake-up and go to sleep, times at which they eat their meals, go out for a walk, and even carry out their personal hygiene. They are also instructed to include any social interactions they may have had during the week, including telephone calls with a friend or acquaintance or time on-line on the Internet. This will provide a profile of how their typical daily functioning unfolds in one week.

Some participants may disclose concerns about suicidal thoughts that are chronic or acute and the leader can lead a discussion within the group about how patients may feel fragile and unable to cope with stress. Such a discussion should be handled with care, but need not be discouraged as long as good clinical judgment is used by the group therapist. It is recommended that the group therapist meets individually with high-risk patients, in order to assess the suicidal risk and take appropriate measures to secure the patient's safety if necessary. Our experience with persistent depression has been that patients with chronic suicidal thoughts often feel more relief than danger from the opportunity provided by the group to share these intrusive thoughts. They may also discover how the suicidal thoughts may be related to maladaptive interpersonal behaviors. The group experience unmistakably breaks the isolation and solitude felt by many patients and encourages patients to see suicide as a maladaptive strategy rather than as some patients may think, the only "solution."

The first two sessions provide an opportunity for group members to express and witness the breadth and depth of theirs and others' mood disorder along with the felt despair associated with the fear that "nothing will ever change." The intensity of these first group sessions usually provides relief to group members who have no one to whom they can express suffering without feeling like a burden. They are encouraged to address all feelings related to death wishes, to feeling misunderstood by others, to feeling inadequate and not useful, to acknowledging maladaptive lifestyles, and to disclosure about the extensive cost of chronic depression in all aspects of their lives. The group therapist assumes an active, supportive role allowing space for these issues to be discussed while keeping the group on task. The therapist sets the stage this way for the group to be a "safe place" where symptoms of chronic depression are discussed openly and their impact on the self and others are explored honestly.

The third group session will add to the narrative of these depressed individuals by helping them understand the "cycle of hopelessness and despair in persistent depression" and thus brings to a climax the initial phase of group treatment in which participants develop cohesion with the awareness of what brings them together. This initial increase of tension and anxiety over the severity of their "dis-ease," isolation, and distress lays the groundwork on which the SA is introduced, at the third session, as a strategy to gain control back over one's life. The SA is meant to have the effect of a negative reinforcement providing relief from the feeling of being disconnected from others and from one's environment due to hopelessness and despair associated with persistent depression. This approach is best understood within an operant conditioning paradigm in which the focus is on new learning acquisition that will help to de-construct or extinguish maladaptive learning within the context of positive interpersonal interactions.

GROUP-CBASP: SESSION 2

Homework review:

Did you bring your Activity Log? If not, here are some extra ones to be filled in now.

Session outline:

- What Interpersonal Domain do you have difficulty with?
- Your Activity Log
- The cycle of depression and inactivity
- Activities:

  - *Taking care of yourself*
  - *Taking care of your environment*
  - *Taking care of your relationships*

- Deal with anxiety that is linked to depression

Today we will begin looking at the consequences of depression on the way you interact socially with others. To do this, we will discuss the one area of your social functioning that you and your therapist selected during the individual session before group began, as a focus for your work in this group. We will call this your Interpersonal Domain. There may be other areas of your social functioning that become more important for you as our work progresses in the group and it is also possible for you to change this Interpersonal Domain to one that becomes a priority.

We will then discuss your daily lifestyle and the way that you spend your time, focusing particularly on your sleep hygiene, eating habits, personal hygiene, daily physical activities, and social activities. We would like to discuss whether you take pleasure in certain activities and what challenges you face.

Homework: For next week, choose a physical and social activity. Plan it and/or try it out. Write it out in your Activity Log (see **Handout 4 in Workbook**) and check it off when you've done it. Assess your mood after the activity.

THE INTERPERSONAL DOMAIN

In the first group session, members share and disclose difficult issues related to their depression and social isolation. This discussion will have set the stage for group members to share with each other, in this second session, their TH (**Handout 3 below**). The TH may be referred to as "the interpersonal or social domain" in order to make it a more useful concept to the group. The group therapist reminds participants that during their individual sessions prior to the beginning of the group, each of them wrote a sentence that identified an Interpersonal Domain with an antecedent such as "If I disclose to others how I feel . . . ," and a consequence "then, they will not take me seriously," for example. The four Interpersonal Domains that represent potential areas of difficulty are:

1. Experiencing closeness with others.
2. Disclosing to others one's needs and feelings.
3. Admitting to making a mistake or to not understanding how to do something.
4. Expressing negative emotions to others.

The group therapist presents to each group member his or her TH written out on a sheet with an invitation to share with others the particular Interpersonal Domain that each will focus on for the duration of this group. Each patient also writes a second sentence that describes one realistic and attainable behavior change that each group member is motivated to make to overcome depression, if they are able to. Some group members may not be ready for this step.

The group therapist may present the TH in a paired-comparisons exercise (see Personal Questionnaire in Part IV, Measuring Skills Acquisition in Group-CBASP), at various times during group therapy. The therapist would present the original TH along with two other revised formulations of the THs that reflect moderate and significant positive change in the TH. The therapist asks group members to rank the TH statements based upon which resonates more with them currently. This is one measure of learned acquisition assessing changes in TH throughout group therapy. This exercise corresponds to indices regarding treatment outcome and is discussed further in the section on Measuring Skills Acquisition in Group-CBASP in Part IV.

HANDOUT 3

YOUR INTERPERSONAL DOMAIN

What is your Interpersonal Domain, as discussed in individual sessions before the group started? Write your sentence here.

_____

If I *(get too close) . . . (express my needs) . . . (make a mistake) . . .* **or** *(express my anger)* **in front of others in the group, then** . . .

_____

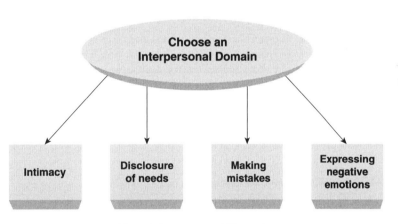

Your Interpersonal Domain

What change in this domain have you identified as being important for you to make? What is the one thing you would like to change about the sentence just above?

The group therapist also explains that in future group sessions the TH, or social domain, of each group member will be distributed on a piece of paper among group members so that each will read the sentence of another in the group whom they will observe more attentively during that session. Group members are instructed to pay attention to times when the person they are observing displays or demonstrates an interpersonal issue related to their identified social domain. The group members draw the group's attention to that social domain and to how it is manifested for a person in the group, at which point the group therapist is able to assist and introduce an IDE if applicable.

Following the discussion on THs, the group reviews the Activity Logs (**Handout 4 in Workbook**) and members discuss their current lifestyle within a typical week. Problematic aspects of their daily routine are identified, particularly with regards to isolation, which results from their avoidance of others. Therapists may vary the contents of this second session to adapt Group-CBASP to a specific patient population (social phobia, PTSD, substance abuse, etc.) and introduce material that is appropriate to address specific issues (such as exposure techniques, relaxation or breathing exercises, or others). Behavioral activation must be addressed and encouraged with persistently depressed patients in order to reinforce that a balanced diet, physical activity, good sleeping habits, attention to personal hygiene, ways to stimulate one's cognitive functioning, and attention to one's environment go hand-in-hand with adaptive interpersonal functioning. The idea of reintroducing positive reinforcements and pleasure experiences, which have been dramatically reduced since the onset of the depressive episode, is discussed and reinforced.

THE CYCLE OF DEPRESSION AND INACTIVITY

Group members are encouraged to choose one problematic area of their personal lifestyle to change. Specifically, they are asked to choose one activity that would represent a challenge for them but that is also a pleasurable or at least a preferred activity. These activities may be in the area of physical exercise, eating or sleeping habits, or in improving personal hygiene. The group leader introduces and explains the concept of graded task assignments. Group members find this to be a positive and reinforcing experience and feel supported by discussing these challenges with peers who understand them.

The members are asked to identify a time in the week when they will begin to put into practice these selected activities or "challenges" for the following week. It may be necessary to discuss issues related to behavioral activation throughout Group-CBASP since realizing these activities assures that patients are improving their quality of life throughout group therapy. Members may need to discuss, typically at the beginning of group sessions, how they were able to carry out the challenge of the previous week and then identify a new level for this challenge for the following week or perhaps identify a new challenge. This discussion often results in members commenting on whether goals set by individuals are realistic and attainable and on how to readjust unrealistic expectations. The opportunity for positive reinforcements given by all group members to each other is also very helpful. Therapists keep the discussion focused on setting a goal and do not allow the discussion to digress for a long time into global, vague, or generalizing descriptions of one's depressive state during the week. However, group members are encouraged to express difficulties carrying out their weekly goals with the purpose of readjusting their graded tasks to make them more realistic and attainable.

Discussions regarding behavioral activation and goal-setting provide therapists with valuable information about how group members cope in their own environment and about possible secondary gains from depression when family members or significant others appear to inadvertently reinforce maladaptive behaviors of persistently depressed and avoidant individuals.

GROUP-CBASP: SESSION 3

Homework review:

Did you bring your Activity Logs? If not, here are some extra ones to be filled in now.

1. What activities did you do or choose to do this past week?

Session outline:

- How maladaptive thinking can lead to maladaptive coping
- The cycle of hopelessness and powerlessness leads to persistent depression
- How can we break the cycle?
- The Situational Analysis (Coping Survey Questionnaire)
- Understanding steps of the Situational Analysis within a group
- Example of a Situational Analysis

The past two sessions have opened our eyes to some of the emotional and physical difficulties you may be experiencing. Some of you may also feel powerless to change and this is why we wanted to suggest some small steps you can take every day to improve your lifestyle and feel healthier physically.

Today, we will also explore how your way of approaching problem situations may contribute to making you feel overwhelmed and unable to get the help you need from others around you.

Homework: For next week, choose an interpersonal situation that you found difficult to manage. Try to complete the Situational Analysis as much as you can and bring it in for the next group.

MALADAPTIVE COGNITIVE AND COPING STRATEGIES OF PERSISTENTLY DEPRESSED PATIENTS

Persistently depressed individuals may have particular difficulty coping with stressful social situations. In fact, the majority of people suffering from a Major Depressive Disorder endorse severe or very severe impairment in the social role domain (Kessler et al., 2003). Recent evidence suggests that depressive severity is associated with being unassertive and submissive with regards to interpersonal efficacy, values, and problems and a less well-rounded pattern of interpersonal functioning or interpersonal rigidity (Locke et al., 2015). In addition, depressed individuals have ruminative (Kuehner & Huffziger, 2012; Lam et al., 2003) and emotion-focused coping styles that exacerbate depressive symptoms. Individuals who have assertive or dominant dispositions regarding interpersonal efficacy, or who have a well-rounded interpersonal profile reflective of a balance and variety of interpersonal behaviors, tend to use more task-focused coping strategies. Depressed patients who do affiliate with others sometimes use social diversion as part of an avoidant coping style which may be more adaptive than emotion-focused coping which tends to intensify negative emotions (Sayegh et al., 2012).

In this third group session, the therapist introduces the cycle of global thinking and defeatism that lead to hopelessness and to loss of control over one's life (**Handout 6 below**). The therapist explains that persistently depressed individuals often use maladaptive coping strategies to deal with stress or daily hassles. CBASP is introduced as a treatment to help these individuals learn to solve interpersonal problems more effectively.

The cycle of persistent depression begins when global thinking is used as a typical approach to coping during an episode of depression. McCullough (2003) makes this very explicit when he explains the way in which depressed individuals describe their problems to others in a global, vague, or over-generalizing manner, such as:

"Nothing will ever work out for me."
"I'll never change."
"No one will ever like me."
"I feel like I'm a worthless person."
"I can't do anything well."
"People always end up rejecting me."

This ***global approach to thinking*** about problems is ineffective as it does not focus attention on any problem in specific and therefore cannot lead to the formulation of a plan of action. Problems are not dealt with and pile up, compounding feelings that nothing will ever change. This global thinking leads the depressed person to feel helpless and to assume a submissive, unassertive position or role in the face of interpersonal adversity or irritation/annoyance from others. This passive position leads to defeatism and self-reproach. ***Defeatist thinking*** is also devaluing of the self and undermines self-confidence with statements such as:

"Why try, nothing I do matters."
"No matter what I do, I will always feel depressed."
"There is no pleasure in anything I do."

Self-defeating thoughts will also never lead to problem resolution but instead will lead to retreat or submission in interactions with others. The depressed person tends to withdraw, feeling powerless as a result of thinking that nothing they do matters to others. Problems are left unresolved and this may elicit in others a complementary reaction, which is to tell the depressed person what to do in order to counteract the helplessness of the depressed patient. Therefore, the defeatist thinking and submissive behaviors of the depressed person draws others, even untrained therapists, into a more dominant role in an attempt to provide the reassurance or support that the depressed person is perceived to need. Sometimes others become hostile toward the depressed person who has adopted a "one-down" position in the face of current problems. These reactions from others are not well received by depressed individuals who often report feeling rejected, misunderstood, unheard, discredited, and sometimes judged negatively by significant others.

Social avoidance and isolation are the result of repeated frustration from unsatisfactory relationships, including with significant others. Group members frequently find that they share similar experiences regarding their tendency to withdraw from others and to favor social isolation. However, prolonged social isolation can result in the depressed person feeling that their behaviors are not important, have no significant impact on others, and that there are therefore ***no consequences to their behavior***. This is when depressed individuals can sometimes convince themselves that their own children would be "better off" without them, or when they begin to feel like a "burden" to others and may experience suicidal thoughts. Feelings of loss of control develop and global thinking that "things will never change" triggers the cycle of hopelessness and powerlessness all over again.

After the group therapist has explained this cycle of global thinking that leads to hopelessness and chronic depression, participants are encouraged to take a few moments and complete their own personal cycle (**Handout 7 in Workbook**). Participants usually have no difficulty describing their own global, generalized thoughts and typical defeatist thinking as well as ways that they each tend to avoid others and withdraw. They also tend to perceive their impact on others as negative or often feel unable to influence the course of events around them due to extensive social isolation. The connection or reciprocity between the individual and his or her environment is severed as a result. Group members share in a discussion of their own experiences with this vicious cycle of persistent depression that leads to loss of control over their lives.

Not all depressed individuals realize that they adopt a submissive or passive position, particularly if their early-onset depression or dysthymia is accompanied by abuse or neglect in childhood. It may be difficult to generate a discussion around their maladaptive tendency to avoid conflict by becoming submissive, since for some this response may have been learned, or conditioned, as the only means to avoid physical or psychological abuse. However, group members have no difficulty identifying global and defeatist thinking and they often all agree about feeling misunderstood by others whose advice is often not seen as helpful. Group members are often able to recognize when significant others inadvertently support their maladaptive behaviors by doing things for them or by excusing them from regular chores or responsibilities, for example. This only serves to reinforce dependency and may contribute to greater anxiety when the depressed person tries to initiate a new activity.

GROUP-CBASP SESSIONS

HANDOUT 6

THE CYCLE OF HOPELESSNESS AND POWERLESSNESS LEADS TO PERSISTENT DEPRESSION

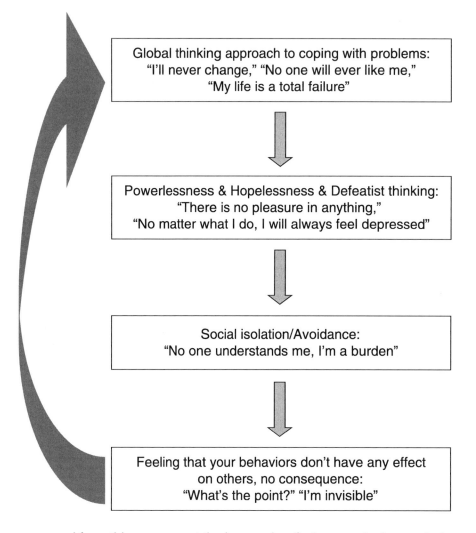

. . . and from this we can get the impression that we are losing control over our lives. **This is how persistent depression can develop . . .**

Adapted from McCullough, J. P., Jr. (2003). *Patient's Manual for CBASP.* New York: The Guilford Press. Copyright Guilford Press. Reprinted with permission of The Guilford Press

The therapist explains that to stop or reverse this vicious cycle of persistent depression the patient must stop using global thinking or over-generalizing as an approach to interpersonal problem situations. Instead, they need to *solve one problem at a time* using a CBASP technique called the *Situational Analysis (SA)*. This technique teaches individuals to focus on one "*slice of time*" within an interpersonal exchange. Patients learn to identify how they influence the outcomes of situations and then learn to look at the consequences of their behaviors. Patients also learn with the supportive help of group members to turn these interpersonal situations around and reach a more desirable outcome.

The therapist uses **Handout 8** provided in the workbook to outline the importance of "*solving one problem at a time*" and to explain the benefits of using the SA. The group then practice using the SA with an example of a difficult interpersonal situation from one of the group members. Group members work together throughout the duration of CBASP group therapy, with situations presented by each group member in turn and discussed openly with the entire group. The procedure used to implement the SA in a group format is presented below.

THE SITUATIONAL ANALYSIS (SA) ADAPTED TO A GROUP MODALITY

The SA comprises a form for the Elicitation Phase (**Handout 9**, **below and in Appendix**) called the Coping Survey Questionnaire (CSQ) by McCullough, adapted to group work in this manual, and a remediation form (**Handout 10 in Session 4 and Appendix**). The first phase, called the Elicitation Phase of the SA, consists of eliciting a description of the interpersonal situation. This description should be concise, focused on behaviors, and consist of a beginning, middle, and end, which are specified as a "*slice of time*." It may be helpful for patients to understand by asking them to think of it as a movie clip that they are describing, where they are a participant in the interaction, but describing it to the group in concrete behavioral terms with a clear start and finish to the clip. The therapist then proceeds to facilitate the remainder of the exercise, and keeps the attention focused on completing the six steps of this phase of the SA. Tension usually rises as members struggle through each of the six steps while resolution of the problem situation in the second remediation phase provides a relief which McCullough identifies as negative reinforcement. It is very important for therapists to **NOT** do the work for any of the group members during the Elicitation Phase but rather to guide them with clear instructions provided at each step. Group members are often very capable of helping each other and this is most effective.

In the second phase, called the Remediation Phase of the SA, the therapist guides the group in a revision of the thoughts and behaviors previously elicited that lead, or not, to the Desired Outcome (DO). The focus here is on identifying an Action Interpretation needed to achieve the DO. Following this phase, the group may decide to do a role-play to practice effective behavioral skills required for the DO.

ELICITATION PHASE OF THE SITUATIONAL ANALYSIS (SA)

For the group SA exercise, the therapist distributes a blank group-SA form (**Handout 9**, **below and in Appendix**) to each member. All members will work together to write down their own answers to each step of the SA that one member is currently reporting upon. Doing the exercise together contributes to the group's cohesion and helps each member learn to formulate a succinct sentence to explain what they mean, which in turn enhances their mentalizing functions. The six steps of the SA are carried out within the group in the following format:

First step of the SA: Describe what happened. This involves a description of an interpersonal situation recounted by one of the group members who is asked to indicate the beginning, middle, and end of the *"slice of time."* The group therapist writes out on a board the member's *exact words* while recounting the event with specific instructions given to *"tell us who said what"* without any editorializing. All other group members write in their own form the description of the situation exactly as it is recounted.

Second step of the SA: Describe your interpretations, your "read" of the situation. The group therapist asks each group member to imagine himself or herself in a similar situation as the one recounted by the presenting group member and to think about how he/she would "interpret" or "read" this situation if he/she had been there in place of the protagonist. The group member reporting the SA (protagonist) also performs this step reflecting on his/her own experience. This step elicits the thoughts or interpretations of the protagonist from the beginning to the end of the *"slice of time"* described, asking group members: *"how did you read what happened?"* A few minutes are spent with each member writing out this second step and a discussion follows beginning with the protagonist who describes his/her interpretations/thoughts about the event, as the group therapist writes this out on the board in the member's own words. All participants are encouraged to formulate complete sentences for this step. The other group members then take turns sharing their interpretations/thoughts, imagining that they had been in such a situation. The therapist keeps the discussion focused within the specific *"slice of time,"* not allowing the discussion to progress to what the protagonist may have done later or to discuss early life traumas or injuries. The discussion needs to stay focused in the **here-and-now** and within the specified *"slice of time."*

Third step of the SA: Describe how you behaved during the situation. The group therapist asks the protagonist to describe his/her own verbal and nonverbal behavior within the *"slice of time"* recounted in step 1, including the tone of voice, eye contact, gesturing, or any other adjective that may describe the observable appearance or actual utterances only. Other group members witness how the protagonist recounted the event observing any nonverbal indicators that are often similar to how the member behaved in the original situation. Group members are able to corroborate the protagonist's description and help by giving their own perception of the protagonist's ***impact*** on them. The group leader writes these behavioral descriptions on the board and members complete the information on their forms in their own words. In this step, group members are focused on the protagonist's behaviors in step 1, not on how they would have imagined their own behavior to be. The group leader may need to clarify these instructions.

Fourth step of the SA: Describe how the event came out for you; the Actual Outcome (AO). All group members are asked to take a moment to think and to write down in a complete sentence, the "**AO**" of the *"slice of time"* recounted by the protagonist. Group members are instructed to describe how the situation ended for the protagonist (not themselves) with a focus on the *"**observable**"* behaviors only and not on theirs or the protagonist's feelings about it. Participants often have difficulty understanding how to provide an **AO** in behavioral terms and time is spent early in Group-CBASP to explain the need to "stick to the facts" and recount only "what happened." The therapist first asks the protagonist to describe how the situation ended for him/her (**AO**), writes it on the board, and then each of the other members' answers are shared. Describing the **AO** is a difficult step for many group members during the initial weeks of Group-CBASP as the tendency is to not pay enough attention to what "actually" happens, that is, to the "facts" of the interpersonal exchange. Participants learn to do SAs through group discussions sharing their own similar experiences to the one introduced by the protagonist. The discussions surrounding steps 4 and 5 are very animated as group members help each other while also trying to formulate and succinctly convey their own thoughts.

Fifth step of the SA: Describe how you wanted the event to come out for you; the DO. The group therapist asks the protagonist how he/she would have liked the situation in step 1 to end; what his/her "**DO**" would be. The protagonist works within the "*slice of time*" previously described while other group members are instructed to think of how **they** would have wanted such a situation to end, **for themselves**, **if they had been in this or in a similar interpersonal situation**; that is their <u>own</u> "**DO**." Group members often misunderstand these instructions and instead suggest how they think the protagonist ought to have behaved or ended the situation, revealing their focus and ability to help others but not themselves. Instructions are given to all group members to identify a realistic and attainable **DO** for themselves in behavioral terms. Emphasis is placed on identifying a goal that can be reached and that the environment can realistically produce, rather than a goal that one wishes ideally to be able to reach or a goal that the environment cannot be guaranteed to produce.

The fifth step of the SA is the most difficult for persistently depressed patients as this is the step that raises the issue of their difficulty identifying an interpersonal motive or goal. Indeed, group members frequently remain silent during step 5, not able to say what they want from one another in the exchange described in step 1. The group discussion is most helpful here to support the protagonist's personal exploration regarding his or her DO. Group members often describe a DO that is not under their control but that depends on the other person in the interaction to whom the protagonist was speaking. Members learn to use the method of Socratic questioning to ask themselves and each other whether it is possible to attain a DO that is not under their control. An example of such a DO is: "I want to make him understand what I am trying to say . . ." The group therapist guides this discussion while keeping it clinically relevant to avoid turning the session into an academic exercise where members become preoccupied with performance or giving the "right answer."

Discussions surrounding the DO often arouse negative emotions regarding the frustrating interpersonal interaction, recounted in step 1. Sometimes the protagonist will not be able to identify a DO, feeling unable to say what he or she wants. This is certainly accepted and normalized by the therapist who turns attention away from the protagonist toward how others in the group would have wanted to end the specific interpersonal interaction recounted in step 1 if they had been in that situation. The therapist facilitates a discussion about the problematic interpersonal conflict raised and about feelings of powerlessness associated with not knowing what one wants. After some time discussing this particular conflict only, the therapist returns again to the protagonist to ask if this discussion helps him/her identify a DO. The therapist keeps the discussion focused on helping the protagonist identify a DO that is under his or her control.

Group members are generally very supportive of each other throughout this process. Nevertheless the protagonist may begin to experience an uncomfortable cognitive dissonance between experiencing, on one hand, a pull to avoid others in the group, due to the patient's own tendency to withdraw, and on the other hand, the positive reinforcement from group members who similarly feel confused or discouraged about having ambiguous or ambivalent interpersonal goals. These discussions gradually move the group members toward a better understanding of what it means to formulate in specific behavioral terms a DO that is under the control of the protagonist and that is attainable. Although the protagonist may identify a DO after a lengthy group discussion, if necessary, this DO may still be reformulated during the Remediation Phase, and the group leader needs to remain open to this possibility.

The role of the group therapist is very critical at this step of group learning and needs to remain focused on highlighting the tense emotional experience of learned helplessness. The therapist also begins to "consequate" the members' interpersonal behaviors during group discussions by pointing out the impact or consequence of their behaviors on each other and on the therapist. As such, the group therapist choreographs the group process to assure that the focus remains on learning goals of CBASP that is learning the nature of one's impact on others. McCullough (2000) clearly outlines the need to follow the sequence of the five-step SA exercise, indicating the rational for each step. This procedure alone assures that the therapist does not "take over" the process and provide the answers, for such dominant behavior on the part of the group leader would inevitably undermine the group members' efforts and struggles to find their own individual solutions.

Sixth step of the SA: Was the DO achieved? Why or why not? These questions are posed to the protagonist once the DO has been formulated to a "satisfactory" degree (it does not need to be perfect or final). The group therapist asks the protagonist: "Did you reach your DO?" McCullough (2000) explains and stresses the importance of this step which brings forth the reasons why, in the protagonist's mind, he or she does not reach the stated DO in this or other similar situations. Emotional tension is often raised within the group as participants share in their frustration about feeling powerless to get what they want from others. If the protagonist answers "no" to this question, the therapist would ask "why not?" and the protagonist usually reports "I don't know" or describes the maladaptive patterns of behaviors that produce the same unsatisfactory outcome he/she feels is not under his/her control: "I never set my limits," "nothing ever works out for me." The protagonist would only answer "yes" to the question if the DO is the same as the AO. This usually occurs when the group is discussing an interpersonal event that was satisfying to the protagonist and did not engender any distress. Such an example may be useful in teaching the SA exercise in the beginning of Group-CBASP or in cases where there is great resistance or fear in the group to discuss any interpersonal conflict. At other times, the group therapist may observe that the protagonist answers "yes" to the question although he/she appears dissatisfied with the DO. It is important to point out to the protagonist and to other observing group members a possible discrepancy between nonverbal behaviors of the protagonist (suggesting dissatisfaction or anger) and the content of the DO. The therapist may ask the protagonist if he/she is satisfied with the DO selected and the answer may change to a "no." The protagonist might explain that he/she feels powerless to do anything else in the situation described in step 1 and this generates more discussion in the group, often uncovering the fact that the protagonist does not know what he or she wants or is too angry about feelings elicited by the situation described in step 1.

The discussion of the interpersonal *"slice of time"* using the structure of the SA naturally engages all group members in a problem-solving exercise that builds group cohesion and individual empowerment. Participants share at each step of the SA and are as involved as the protagonist in identifying their own answers.

An example of a completed SA is found in the Appendix.

HANDOUT 9

THE SITUATIONAL ANALYSIS (SA)
(FOR GROUP THERAPY)

(Coping Survey Questionnaire—CSQ)

Your Name: _____

Name of person reporting the situation: _____

Therapist: _____

Date of Situational Event: _____

Date of Therapy Session: _____

Instructions: Select one stressful interpersonal event that you have confronted during the past week and describe it using the format below. Please try to fill out <u>all</u> parts of the form. Your therapist will assist you in reviewing this Situational Analysis during your next therapy session.

Situational Area: Family____   Work/School____   Social____

Step 1. Describe <u>WHAT</u> happened: (Write who said or did what, then describe clearly how the interpersonal event ended—the final point.)
Note to group members: *The person reporting the situation speaks, the other group members write down what he or she said about the situation.*

Adapted to group therapy from: J.P. McCullough, Jr. (2000). *Treatment for Chronic Depression: Cognitive Behavioral Analysis System of Psychotherapy (CBASP)*. New York: Guilford Press, page 107. Adapted with permission of The Guilford Press

HANDOUT 9

Step 2. How did you <u>INTERPRET</u> what happened during the event? (How do you "read" what happened; what thoughts did you have which indicate how the interpersonal event unraveled from the beginning to the end of this exchange? Make a sentence for each interpretation. Try to limit yourself to three interpretations.)

Note to group members: If the situation in step 1 is not yours but that of another group member, then imagine yourself in a similar situation and write a thought that you might have experienced in such an exchange. Write at least one sentence.

a. _____

_____

b. _____

_____

c. _____

_____

Step 3. Describe what you <u>DID</u> during the situation, your behaviors: (How did you say what you said? What were some of your nonverbal behaviors, tone of voice, eye contact, etc?)

Note to group members: We are describing here the behaviors of the person reporting the situation in step 1 (name the person), we are not describing the behaviors of other group members in their imagined situations. How do you think she or he behaved in the situation in Step 1?

Step 4. Describe <u>HOW</u> the event came out for <u>You</u> (The <u>ACTUAL OUTCOME</u> (AO)): (What *ACTUALLY* happened at the end of this exchange; what was observable? Write one complete sentence describing observable behaviors.)

Note to group members: Now we are looking at the AO for the person who reported the situation in step 1 (name the person). In your own words, how did the situation end for her/him?

Adapted to group therapy from: J.P. McCullough, Jr. (2000). *Treatment for Chronic Depression: Cognitive Behavioral Analysis System of Psychotherapy (CBASP)*. New York: Guilford Press, page 107. Adapted with permission of The Guilford Press

HANDOUT 9

Step 5. Describe how you <u>Wanted</u> the event to come out for you (The <u>DESIRED OUTCOME</u> (DO)): (How would you have <u>WANTED</u> the event to come out for you? What <u>goal</u> would you have wanted to achieve, that is realistic, attainable and depends on you? Describe it in behavioral terms using a complete sentence.
Note to group members: Here, again, if the situation in step 1 is not yours, then imagine yourself in the same situation as you did in step 2 and now think of <u>your</u> DO for <u>yourself</u>. How would <u>you</u> have wanted the situation to end if <u>you</u> were there?

Step 6. Did you get what you wanted? YES___ NO___ Why or why not?
Explain why you think you do not get what you want in similar situations:
Note to group members: Every group member can also think about whether he or she would get what he or she wants in a similar situation.

_____
_____
_____
_____
_____

After the Remediation Phase of the exercise, identify:
<u>My Action Interpretation</u>: Write out a thought that you need to tell yourself (like a coach speaking to you in your head) that will help you reach your goal, your DO, in this particular interpersonal situation described in step 1.
Note to group members: Even if the situation is not yours in step 1, think about what your internal coach needs to tell you to reach your own DO.

_____
_____
_____
_____
_____

Adapted to group therapy from: J.P. McCullough, Jr. (2000). *Treatment for Chronic Depression: Cognitive Behavioral Analysis System of Psychotherapy (CBASP)*. New York: Guilford Press, page 107. Adapted with permission of The Guilford Press

GROUP-CBASP: SESSION 4

Homework review:

1. What activities did you do this past week?
2. Did you bring in a copy of the Situational Analysis with a difficult situation to discuss?

Session outline:

- The Remediation Phase of the Situational Analysis
- What is a Future Situational Analysis

Homework: For next week, choose an interpersonal situation that you found difficult to manage. Try to complete the Situational Analysis as much as you can and bring it in for the next group. We will do the Remediation Phase together.

REMEDIATION PHASE OF THE SITUATIONAL ANALYSIS (SA)

Following the six steps of the Elicitation Phase of the SA in Group-CBASP, the group leader introduces the Remediation Phase (**Handout 10 below**) of the SA involving the steps below to reach an Action Interpretation that best prepares the person to realize their DO. The Action Interpretation is like an inner coach using a positive self-statement to move the person to action.

> **First step of Remediation:** After the Elicitation Phase of the SA is completed, and the DO is identified, described in behavioral terms, and determined to be realistic and attainable, the Remediation Phase of SA is conducted. The group leader ensures that the group understands the situation presented and, if appropriate, the dilemma contained in the situation, including maladaptive patterns of behavior that prevent the protagonist from reaching his/her DO. The group therapist then suggests that the protagonist and others in the group turn their attention to the interpretations in step 2 of the SA to see if these would help the protagonist reach his/her DO or not.

McCullough (2000) describes the resolution of the Remediation Phase as being a negative reinforcement experience. Specifically, the heightened distress and helplessness are at their highest at the end of the Elicitation Phase when the AO and Desired Outcome do not match and patients do not know why they don't reach their DO or "get what they want." Some individuals feel as though they cannot find a meaningful way forward and the Remediation Phase will resolve this tension with a positive experience of learning to identify realistic and attainable goals. Understanding is gained regarding how to move toward their achieving goals with an Action Interpretation and adaptive behaviors.

During remediation, the therapist asks the protagonist and others in the group to review each interpretation of the SA and consider whether each one is ***relevant to and grounded in*** the situation described in step 1, meaning that the statement is pertinent to the situation and to the facilitation of the DO and is based upon the specific current situation and not based upon global or past situations. The therapist also asks if the interpretations are ***accurate or true***, that is, do they reflect the reality of the situation in step 1. Group members explore and discuss these questions and ask themselves if the interpretations provided by the protagonist and group members are ***grounded*** in the event, in that each interpretation ought to "reflect what actually happened in the slice of time." If this is the case, then the interpretation is said to be ***relevant***. "Teaching a patient to 'read' accurately the ongoing flow involved in interpersonal encounters plants the person's perceptual 'feet' solidly in the moment," according to McCullough (2000, p. 114). Also, the interpretation is ***accurate*** if it describes what actually happened between the protagonist and others within the given slice of time, rather than reflecting only the feelings, thoughts, or perceptions of the protagonist or past or future events or situations.

- If the interpretation is ***grounded***, ***relevant***, and ***accurate*** then the group therapist will suggest keeping it and asks how this interpretation helps the protagonist reach his/her DO. If the interpretation doesn't help reach the DO, it is not incorporated further in the discussion, even if it may have been relevant and accurate.
- The DO may be revised at this step of the remediation if the protagonist acknowledges that it is not attainable or realistic. Otherwise, the same exercise is done to revise each of the remaining interpretations listed for the particular SA.

Second step of Remediation: The second step in the revision of the SA is to construct, if necessary, an *Action Interpretation*, which is a self-generated thought that is a cognitive precursor to assertive behavior. The Action Interpretation may be present but not fully articulated or may be absent and it is the cognitive work that prepares the protagonist for behavior which will facilitate achievement of the DO. The group therapist asks the protagonist: "What do you need to say to yourself about what you need to do to reach your DO, your goal?" Other group members are often very helpful and supportive of the protagonist and all work together to find a self-statement that will help him/her reach the desired interpersonal goal consisting of a behavior to carry out.

Third step of Remediation: The group therapist then asks the protagonist: "If you had this Action Interpretation in your mind during this interpersonal situation in step 1 of the SA, how would your behavior have changed (in that slice of time)?" The protagonist needs to answer this question first and may reveal an insightful statement, especially if he/she has been able to do the SA from beginning to end.

Fourth step of Remediation: The group therapist then asks: "If you had behaved in this new way you describe, would you have gotten what you wanted, that is, your DO?" Again, the protagonist will often disclose important insight onto the consequences of his or her actions.

Fifth step of Remediation: Finally, the group therapist asks the protagonist and other group members: "What did you learn today doing this exercise?" The group leader may pose additional questions to help facilitate generalization of learning, such as "Can you think of any other interactions where what you learned today applies?" or "Has anything similar to this happened with anyone else in your life?" This step is meant to further consolidate learning and promote generalization of learning. McCullough (2000) underlines the importance of allowing the protagonist to think and identify the learning that took place and most importantly the behaviors that need to change in order for a person to reach his/her interpersonal goals. It may take time for group members to name what they learned and more practice with the SA may help, however hearing other group members' learning experience is also very helpful. Often group members will point out an important aspect of the SA that the protagonist didn't give himself/herself credit for.

Once the SA is completed, and the AO=DO, the group can celebrate and reinforce the achievement! Positive reinforcement is important to help consolidate learning and make sure that the persistently depressed patients do not miss "the good stuff!" The group may also take time after the completion of the group SA to practice social skills-training and learn interpersonal skills through role-plays and in-vivo exposure with other group members, practicing new behaviors and further consolidating learning.

Once all the steps of the Elicitation and Remediation Phases of the SA have been discussed in the group setting, all participants will have had a first-hand experience with this problem-solving strategy. The group therapist collects the members' completed SA forms at the end of each group session. These forms will be used to monitor learning over the course of Group-CBASP and contribute to a clinical profile for each group member. Copies may be given to group members to help them review their work.

HANDOUT 10

SITUATIONAL ANALYSIS (SA): REMEDIATION PHASE

Now, let's go back into the situation that you described in step 1 of your SA and see what you might have changed to get what you wanted.

Step 1:

A- We first look at your interpretations. In the first interpretation, you said . . .

- Is this interpretation <u>grounded</u> in the event? Does the interpretation reflect what actually happened in this situation? If so, it is a relevant interpretation. A relevant interpretation plants your feet solidly in the event and helps achieve your DO.
- Is this interpretation true or <u>accurate</u>? I mean, do you think the interpretation accurately describes what is happening between you and the other person, or something that is happening in you: your feelings, thoughts, etc.?

<u>Rule</u>: If your interpretation is relevant and accurate, we will keep it. If it is relevant but not accurate, we will modify it. If it is neither relevant nor accurate, we will not address it further, and instead accept that it is not helpful in achieving your DO.

- Finally, how does this interpretation help you get to your Desired Outcome, that is, to what you want in that situation? If it doesn't help you get there, can we eliminate it?

<u>Rule</u>: If you now find that your Desired Outcome is unattainable or unrealistic after revising an interpretation, you need to revise the Desired Outcome first before continuing.

Now do the same with the second and third interpretations . . .

B- Now you may need an *ACTION INTERPRETATION*, which will prepare you to move toward getting what you want. This is a thought that you say to yourself about what you need to do to reach your Desired Outcome, your goal.

Step 2:

Now that you have revised your interpretations and perhaps found an *Action Interpretation*, how would your behavior have changed if you had used these revised or new interpretations?

If you had behaved this way, would you have gotten what you wanted, that is, your DO?

© J.P. McCullough, Jr. (2000). *Treatment for Chronic Depression: Cognitive Behavioral Analysis System of Psychotherapy (CBASP)*. New York: Guilford Press, pp. 282–284. Copyright of Guilford Press. Reprinted with permission of The Guilford Press

USING A FUTURE SITUATIONAL ANALYSIS (SA)

The SA may be typically utilized early in therapy to describe and remediate *past* events, but may also be used to plan and rehearse upcoming or hypothetical *future* events. The format for using the SA for anticipated events includes three steps that must be completed by the patient (**Handout 11 in Appendix**):

1. Identify the Desired Outcome (in behavioral terms) for the future event.
2. Identify what interpretations, especially the "action reads," are necessary to achieve the DO.
3. Identify the behaviors that must be enacted in order to achieve the DO.

Conducting future event SAs will help the patient feel more prepared to manage interpersonal events successfully and further generalize learning and perceived functionality, as well as increase the number of positive events and interactions in the patient's life.

GROUP-CBASP: SESSION 5

Homework review:

1. What activities did you do this past week?
2. Did you bring in a copy of the Situational Analysis with a difficult situation to discuss?

Session outline:

PRACTICING THE SITUATIONAL ANALYSIS (SA) WITH ELICITATION AND REMEDIATION PHASES

- Using the Situational Analysis to understand the impact of our interpersonal behaviors on others within or outside the group

This session is devoted to practicing Situational Analyses with Elicitation and Remediation Phases. We will repeat this exercise for many sessions throughout group therapy.

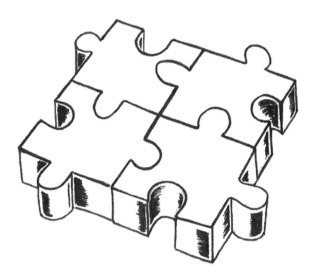

Homework: For next week, choose an interpersonal situation that you found difficult to manage. Try to complete the Situational Analysis as much as you can and bring it in for the next group. We will do the Remediation Phase together.

GROUP-CBASP: SESSION 6

Homework review:

1. What activities did you do this past week?
2. Did you bring in a copy of the Situational Analysis with a difficult situation to discuss?

Session outline:

- Your Interpersonal Domain
- How is this Domain expressed with others in this group?
- Using the Interpersonal Domain to understand the impact within the group of our interpersonal behaviors
- Is this your DO?

Homework: For next week, choose an interpersonal situation that you found difficult to manage. Try to complete the Situational Analysis as much as you can and bring it in for the next group. We will do the Remediation Phase together.

HANDOUT 12

YOUR INTERPERSONAL DOMAIN

The therapist guides a discussion about the TH and any changes observed by group members themselves or by others observing them in the group regarding the TH. This is also an opportunity to measure progress made using the Personal Questionnaire discussed in Part IV on Measuring Skills Acquisition in Group-CBASP or using any other measure. Specifically, it is important to assess the degree to which group members believe the TH that they wrote about themselves before beginning group therapy. This discussion about change and progress often provides opportunities for self-disclosure, thanks, in part, to growing group cohesion. The therapist may seize an opportunity here to do an IDE pointing out the risks that members take and the impacts on group members compared to the impacts on a malevolent significant other from the patient's past or current life. The therapist deliberately initiates the discussion with the following:

Let's look again at your Interpersonal Domain, at the sentence you constructed about what behaviors you avoid in your interactions with others. Write your sentence here:

_____

_____

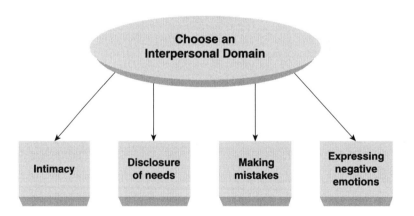

What change in this domain have you identified as being important for you to make? What is the one thing you would like to change about the sentence just above?

_____

_____

_____

_____

The therapist draws attention to current behaviors within the group and to the increased cohesion and therapeutic alliances between group members. This is another example of the use of Disciplined Involvement described earlier in Part II of Group-CBASP methodology. The therapist shares his or her understanding of the impact value of each group member on himself/herself and on others in or outside the group, encouraging feedback between group members about their mutual impacts on each other. It is also possible to discuss how skills learned within the group can be generalized to interpersonal situations outside the group, including marital relationships, conflicts at work, or social isolation. The therapist may use the following exploratory questions to discuss how participants' behaviors within the group impact others and how this may be largely due to their feared interpersonal domain.

To do this, the group explores how each person may use maladaptive behaviors to protect the self from the feared consequence of the Interpersonal Domain. Some patients report: "I never say no," "I never call back friends," or "I don't know what to say so I'm silent." Others in the group can confirm that the impact of "I never say no" on themselves might be negative and lead to rejection due to a dislike of someone who is overly accommodating. The impact of "I never call back friends" might be to appear disinterested in the friends and hence the therapist may suggest that the person might also appear disinterested within the group. The impact of "I don't know what to say so I'm silent" might be to appear to push others away. Group members reflect on whether the impact they have on others agrees with their values and self-image. If not, the door to change is opened.

Do you notice how your behaviors in this group reflect the Interpersonal Domain that you have the most trouble with?

- Have you yet shown others your feelings or needs? (disclosure)
- Have you yet allowed others to get to know you? (intimacy)
- Have you yet acknowledged to others your difficulties, weaknesses? (making mistakes)
- Have you expressed some negative feelings that you are experiencing? (expressing negative emotions)

Do you think you <u>have</u> taken any risks here in the group by expressing one of the four Interpersonal Domains? If yes, then how difficult was it for you to do it?

1   5   10

Not difficult - **Very difficult**

_____

_____

_____

_____

How would an important person in your life who has misunderstood or abused you (a Significant Other) have responded to you if you had taken this risk in front of him or her?

_____

_____

_____

_____

How have we responded to you in the group when you took this risk?

_____

_____

_____

_____

What is different about _what_ you experienced with your Significant Other and _what_ you have experienced here with us?

_____

_____

_____

_____

What meaning will this have for you if we can respond differently to you here and now? What do you learn from this?

_____

_____

_____

_____

If you think you haven't taken any risks and not expressed any of the four Interpersonal Domains in the group or outside, then what behaviors do you use to protect yourself from the consequences you imagine getting from others in the Domain that is most difficult for you?

_____

_____

_____

_____

Do these behaviors agree with your values? Is this how you want to live your life? Does this help your mood?

_____

_____

_____

_____

What impact do you have on others around you with these protective behaviors? You can ask group members how they see you. What is that one thing you want to change about the impact you have on others?

_____

_____

_____

_____

Now think about your DO when you use protective behaviors. Are you getting what you want from others? Is the protective behavior more important for you than what you want in an interpersonal exchange?

_____

_____

_____

_____

GROUP-CBASP: SESSIONS 7 & 8

Homework review:

1. What activities did you do this past week?
2. Did you bring in a copy of the Situational Analysis with a difficult situation to discuss?

Session outline:

PRACTICING THE SITUATIONAL ANALYSIS (SA) WITH ELICITATION AND REMEDIATION PHASES

• Using the Situational Analysis to understand the impact of our interpersonal behaviors on others within or outside the group

These sessions are devoted to practicing Situational Analyses. The therapist is attentive to times when a "hot spot" emerges in the discussion, related to the Transference Hypothesis, and elicits reactions from group members about the impact of maladaptive or adaptive behaviors on others, as was explained in the previous session. The therapist uses Disciplined Personal Involvement with either an Interpersonal Discrimination Exercise (IDE) or Contingent Personal Responsivity (CPR) to emphasize learning about the impact each has on the other. Please see examples of Contingent Personal Responsivity in sessions 13 and 14.

Homework: For next week, choose an interpersonal situation that you found difficult to manage. Try to complete the Situational Analysis as much as you can and bring it in for the next group. We will do the Remediation Phase together.

GROUP-CBASP: SESSIONS 9 & 10

Homework review:

1. What activities did you do this past week?
2. Did you bring in a copy of the Situational Analysis with a difficult situation to discuss?

Session outline:

- Understanding our interpersonal interactions
- Your Interpersonal Circumplex

    - *Your Interpersonal Values*
    - *Your Interpersonal Efficacy*

- How is your interpersonal profile related to your interpersonal behaviors within this group?
- Eight Styles of Interpersonal Relating

Homework: For next week, choose an interpersonal situation that you found difficult to manage. Try to complete the Situational Analysis as much as you can and bring it in for the next group. We will do the Remediation Phase together.

THE INTERPERSONAL CIRCUMPLEX IN GROUP-CBASP

The Interpersonal Circumplex or circle (IPC) is a useful model to help group members visualize their interpersonal functioning on a circular diagram to help see the impact of their behaviors on others. Like CBASP, this model conveys an interpersonal explanation of depression and explores dimensions and constructs of interpersonal motivation, self-efficacy, and behavior (Pincus & Wright, 2011). This model complements CBASP and facilitates an understanding of the maladaptive functioning of persistently depressed patients within their current interpersonal environment.

One objective of the Interpersonal Circumplex as used in Group-CBASP is to provide education regarding interpersonal interactions. Group members learn about and discuss common principles about interactions between people such as what motivates people to interact, what a complementary or non-complementary response is, and how interactions come to be conflictual or frustrating. The importance of making one's motives clear in an interaction with another person reinforces the need to clarify what one wants from the other. With such knowledge, group members are better able to anticipate the type of interpersonal conflicts they are most likely to experience as a result of their own interpersonal style, and this can be visually depicted on the Interpersonal Circumplex.

A strategy to prevent this session from becoming too didactic and theoretical is to provide group members with results of questionnaires that they will have completed at the beginning of Group-CBASP, some of which are outlined below. These results are hand-scored and the scores placed on an Interpersonal Circumplex for each participant. The scores reveal each group member's preferred style of relating or what is called their interpersonal disposition. The group therapist can describe the Interpersonal Circumplex model while group members examine their own personal profile.

The Interpersonal Circumplex depicted (see **Figure 1**) reflects the relationship between two categories of interpersonal behaviors, traits, or motives. On the horizontal axis the dimension of *Affiliation* represents the need for closeness or communion with others at one end of the continuum and the need for distance from others at the other end. Behaviors that seek closeness with others, belonging, loss of boundaries when too close to others, cooperation and union with others are observed along this continuum. On the vertical axis the dimension of *Agency* portrays the sense of having control, dominance or power over one's life, with dominance at one end and submissiveness at the other end. Assertive behaviors, behaviors that attempt to influence others, competitive or dominating behaviors are all observed along this continuum. These two dimensions represent the two challenges which we are faced with since childhood; that is the need to get along with others and the need to move forward in life with independence and autonomy (Horowitz et al., 2006).

The group therapist can introduce the Interpersonal Circumplex as a visual tool to better understand how our interactions are most often motivated by what we want from each other and by how we get what we want, as described in the patient's workbook. The interpersonal style of an individual can be understood by examining four different aspects of interpersonal interactions:

1. The individual's interpersonal wishes and fears represented by **interpersonal values** (Locke, 2000) (**Handout 13 in Appendix**);
2. The individual's beliefs about what interpersonal behaviors he or she can or cannot do, indicative of **interpersonal efficacy** (Locke & Sadler, 2007) (**Handout 14 in Appendix**);
3. The individual's reported distress about **interpersonal problems** or behaviors

he or she does too much or not enough (Horowitz, Alden, Wiggins, & Pincus, 2000) (**Handout 15 in Workbook**);

4. The **impact** or influence of the individual's interpersonal behaviors on how others perceive or feel about him or her (Kiesler & Schmidt, 1993).

Assessing an individual's interpersonal style and dispositions with the above-mentioned circumplex scales yields a particular interpersonal configuration for each person along eight octants. **Table 1 (Handout 19 below)** outlines the eight interpersonal styles with corresponding characteristics for each of the four scales previously described. All four scales are easily hand-scored to obtain means that are placed on the eight octants of the circumplex for each group participant. Each person's predominant style in the submissive, dominant, friendly, or distant quadrants can be plotted visually. Participants can now see how their predominant interpersonal disposition may contribute to difficulties obtaining a DO in their interactions with others. Information can also be obtained on the degree of interpersonal rigidity or adaptability as well as interpersonal distress using the same circumplex scales.

Group members discuss together their own interpersonal style as depicted on the circumplex using their own results to the above-mentioned scales. The impact on others of each individual's interpersonal style is more easily visualized using the Interpersonal Circumplex, particularly when the complementary nature of interactions is explained at the next session. The therapist and group members can then question each other more easily about the benefits of interpersonal behaviors or coping strategies that may be seen as maladaptive due to their position on the circumplex.

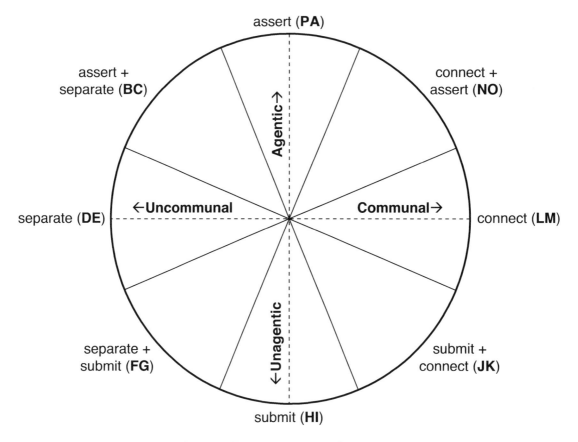

Figure 1 The Interpersonal Circumplex
Locke (2006, 2011)

GROUP-CBASP: SESSIONS 9 & 10   **63**

HANDOUT 19

EIGHT STYLES OF INTERPERSONAL RELATING

The Interpersonal Circumplex has **eight styles** depicting typical modes of interacting that result from the combination of the two dimensions of *Agency* and *Affiliation* (Locke, 2006, 2011). These are the following:

Table 1 Eight Styles of Interpersonal Relating

Style	Interpersonal Values "It is important that I . . ." (Locke, 2000)	Interpersonal Efficacy "I am confident that I can . . ." (Locke & Sadler, 2007)	Interpersonal Problems "I am too . . ." (Horowitz et al., 2000)	Interpersonal Impacts "When I am with this person, he/she makes me feel . . ." (Kiesler & Schmidt, 1993)
Dominant (Assert)	appear confident, correct, in authority	be assertive, forceful, take charge, speak when I have something to say	domineering/controlling	bossed around
Dominant & Distant (Assert & Separate)	appear forceful, have the upper hand, avenge any attacks or insults	be aggressive if needed, keep the upper hand, tell them when I am annoyed, win an argument or competition	vindictive/self-centered	that I want to stay away from him/her
Distant (Separate)	appear cool and detached, be guarded and conceal my thoughts and feelings	be cold and unfriendly when I want to, be cruel or tough when the situation calls for it, get them to leave me alone	cold/distant	distant from him/her
Yielding & Distant (Separate & Submit)	avoid ridicule and rejection by avoiding blunders or concealing my feelings	be quiet, submissive, disappear into the background when I want, hide my thoughts and feelings	socially inhibited	that I should tell him/her not to be so nervous around me
Yielding (Submit)	avoid arguments and anger by going along with what others want and expect	avoid getting into arguments, avoid making them angry, be a follower, let others take charge	non-assertive	in charge

Table 1 continued

Style	Interpersonal Values "It is important that I . . ." (Locke, 2000)	Interpersonal Efficacy "I am confident that I can . . ." (Locke & Sadler, 2007)	Interpersonal Problems "I am too . . ." (Horowitz et al., 2000)	Interpersonal Impacts "When I am with this person, he/she makes me feel . . ." (Kiesler & Schmidt, 1993)
Yielding & Friendly (Submit & Connect)	get others to like and approve of me by putting others' needs first	be giving, nice, follow the rules, get along with others	overly accommodating	that I could tell him/her anything and he/she would agree
Friendly (Connect)	feel connected with, genuinely cared about and supported by others	be helpful, fit in, soothe hurt feelings, understand others' feelings	self-sacrificing	appreciated by him/her
Dominant & Friendly (Connect & Assert)	express myself openly, be heard, respected, have an impact	be a leader, express myself openly, get others to listen to what I have to say, smooth over difficulties	intrusive/needy	that I could relax and he/she'd take charge

GROUP-CBASP: SESSIONS 11 & 12

Homework review:

1. What activities did you do this past week?
2. Did you bring in a copy of the Situational Analysis with a difficult situation to discuss?

Session outline:

- Your Interpersonal Circumplex—Inventory of Interpersonal Problems
- Understanding extreme scores of interpersonal conflict
- What typical behaviors would you use to reach your goals; think of what you have done in the past, your AO?
- Understanding some typical interpersonal patterns of individuals with persistent depression
- Do you think you are more rigid or flexible in your interpersonal interactions?
- What are the consequences of interpersonal avoidance for you?

Homework: For next week, choose an interpersonal situation that you found difficult to manage. Try to complete the Situational Analysis as much as you can and bring it in for the next group. We will do the Remediation Phase together.

USING AN INTERPERSONAL PROFILE IN GROUP-CBASP

In these group sessions, the therapist encourages a discussion around scores obtained on the scale measuring interpersonal problems (Horowitz et al., 2000) (**Handout 15 in Workbook**), or any other similar scale used to assess interpersonal distress. Extreme scores are explained and the tendency for depression to be associated with unassertive and overly accommodating behaviors is discussed, as these behaviors have been observed in the AOs that were described in SAs of group members. Any difficulties group members have had doing SAs, particularly finding an appropriate DO, can be discussed now in the context of problematic interpersonal situations. Using the eight quadrants of the circumplex can help patients visualize and understand some of these interpersonal problems and adaptive or maladaptive behaviors used to get what they want in interactions with others. A discussion of coping strategies patients use when they repeatedly do not get what they want can be useful to help them understand the impact they have on others.

The Interpersonal Circumplex is used to emphasize the importance of bidirectional communication between two individuals and how this communication breaks down. Horowitz et al. (2006) provide a very useful model to understand how interpersonal motives are at the center of interpersonal interactions using the dimensions of *Agency* and *Affiliation*. These researchers explain that the meaning of an interpersonal behavior largely depends on the objective or motive underlying it. When the motive is clear, the interpersonal behavior is often also easy to understand and when the motive is not clear, the behavior is often ambiguous. This type of ambiguous behavior leads to misunderstandings and sometimes to feelings of distress. Depressed individuals often don't realize the problematic nature of their AO in specific unsatisfactory interpersonal situations. However, other group members quickly identify maladaptive behaviors of others in the group and give accurate feedback about the impact of these behaviors on themselves or on the person within the situation described.

Depressed individuals sometimes have two or more motives in mind during one interpersonal interaction and these motives may either conflict with each other or one may be hidden while the other displayed. For example, an individual may want to influence another but fears being seen as controlling, therefore will withdraw. The fear takes precedence over the need to influence and the individual may feel frustrated or disappointed. On the other hand, exercising influence or power over another might alienate a friendship if the behavior is maladaptive. The therapist and group members discuss the importance of making motives clear both to oneself and to the other person in a dyad. When the other responds in the way that is expected, then we are likely to feel satisfied.

Similar to the Interpersonal Circumplex, CBASP also frames interpersonal interactions in terms of their reciprocity or bidirectional nature. CBASP enables the depressed person to understand the maladaptive interpersonal behaviors within and negative consequences of their AOs. CBASP also enables the depressed person to identify and accurately verbally convey realistic and attainable DOs regarding what he/she wants from the other. The depressed patient learns how interpersonal conflict can result from their own frustrated or vague motives, which may be the consequence or impact of maladaptive interpersonal behaviors observed in the AO.

The work of Group-CBASP involves helping the depressed person formulate a "DO" that is attainable and under his or her control and that takes into consideration the possibility that the other person may refuse to respond in the expected way. This refusal may generate frustration within the depressed person whose consequent reactions or coping mechanisms may be maladaptive (Horowitz et al., 2006). Group-CBASP is introduced as an opportunity to learn social problem-solving strategies such as that of the SA to reach desired interpersonal goals that are realistic and attainable and to have the desired impact on one's environment, and thus helps engender a feeling of control over one's life. This is the very nature of bidirectional interpersonal reciprocity.

GROUP-CBASP: SESSIONS 13 & 14

Homework review:

1. What activities did you do this past week?
2. Did you bring in a copy of the Situational Analysis with a difficult situation to discuss?

Session outline:

- What are complementary and non-complementary interactions?
- Are you getting what you want from others?
- Do your hidden motives push others away?
- What is your DO?
- Examples of Contingent Personal Responsivity in Group-CBASP

Homework: For next week, choose an interpersonal situation that you found difficult to manage. Try to complete the Situational Analysis as much as you can and bring it in for the next group. We will do the Remediation Phase together.

COMPLEMENTARY AND NON-COMPLEMENTARY INTERACTIONS

According to Horowitz et al. (2006), in our interactions with others we usually seek to elicit, invite, or evoke a response or a reaction from another person that we want or expect and that will fulfill our motive or goal. The other's response is called the "<u>complement</u>" of the behavior we emit. If the other person responds to you in the way that you expect, then the response is said to be complementary and you are likely to feel satisfied.

- *The **complement** of a behavior is the reaction from the other that satisfies the motive or goal underlying your behavior.*

  - *A behavior and its complement are **similar** with respect to the horizontal dimension: Friendliness invites friendliness and distance invites distance.*
  - *A behavior and its complement are **reciprocal** with respect to the vertical dimension: Control invites submission and submission invites control.*

If the other person responds to you in a way that does not meet your expectations, then this response is said to be non-complementary.

- *A **non-complementary** behavior is one that does not satisfy your motive or goal with that person.*

(Horowitz et al., 2006)

Horowitz et al. (2006) reformulated Kiesler's model of interpersonal *complementarity* in light of evidence of the high frequency of friendly reactions to hostile behavior. These findings do not confirm the principle of complementarity that was previously elaborated, particularly regarding hostile behaviors, and have lead Horowitz to introduce the concept of "motive" or "goal" on the part of person A in initiating an interpersonal interaction with person B to better explain this theoretical problem. The revised model suggests that a focus on person A's motive in interacting with person B would mean that A *invites* a "desired" reaction or behavior from person B which in turn person B may choose to refuse, for whatever reason. Person B's reaction is complementary if it is the "desired" reaction or behavior which A would like to obtain from B and which would satisfy A's motive. Person A is likely satisfied when B responds in the way that A expects and A is likely dissatisfied or even frustrated when B does not respond in the expected direction. This revised model allows many facets of motivation to come into play between persons A and B such as the possibility that person A may not be aware of his or her motives regarding person B and that these motives may serve a need to protect the self from feared consequences in interactions with B.

Furthermore, one may accurately interpret someone else's motive but decide to reply with a non-complementary behavior, that is, a behavior that does not meet the other's expectations. When important motives are frustrated, negative feelings result that may bring about interpersonal problems for one or for two people in a dyad. Persistently depressed individuals often report problems that result from interpersonal motives that are often frustrated, such as "No one understands me" or "I'm often alone."

There are also interpersonal motives that serve to protect a weak or vulnerable self (Horowitz et al., 2006). Individuals devise strategies to satisfy these motives as well but may not always be aware of how they go about doing this. For example, a person may have learned to reject others before being rejected or abandoned. Such a person may have developed a personality style in which the predominant motive is one aimed at self-protection. When these self-protective strategies fail and the motive is frustrated, negative feelings result and individuals resort to coping behaviors to deal with these feelings. Persistently depressed individuals often develop maladaptive coping behaviors such as oversleeping, overeating, abusing drugs or alcohol. Social isolation is also a common maladaptive response to interpersonal difficulties among the persistently depressed.

In light of Horowitz et al.'s revised interpersonal model placing the satisfaction or frustration of agentic (otherwise called dominant) or communal motives at the center of interpersonal interactions, the DO of the SA within the CBASP model becomes a prime example of such a central motive. The DO can also be situated within one of the four octants of the Interpersonal Circumplex and examined with regards to whether it is attainable and realistic in a particular interpersonal situation. Then the complementary response to this DO can also be identified on the circumplex along with its impact on the respondent.

This model places CBASP's DO, within an interpersonal interaction, as center-stage with a focus on identifying the depressed patient's particular goal in each interpersonal interaction with others and the typical behaviors used to reach this goal. Then, the depressed patient considers the "desired" reaction or behavior from the other (along the broad dimensions of Agency and Affiliation) that would satisfy his or her DO. A complementary reaction from the other is one that fulfills the stated DO or interpersonal goal and results in satisfaction for the depressed patient. On the other hand, a non-complementary response is one that would result in the frustration of the stated goal or DO due to a reaction from the other that is not "desired." This reminds depressed individuals of the reciprocal nature of interpersonal interactions and of the mutual consequences each have on the other and opens the door to a discussion of adaptive coping strategies when we don't get what we want from others.

When a withdrawn group member explains, for example, that his or her DO of avoiding social contact is related to fear of disclosing feelings or needs to others, the therapist may ask if avoidant behaviors were learned as a way to protect the self, and now avoiding others may be contributing to social isolation which, in turn, maintains depression. Participants cannot deny that their presence in the group is motivated by a need to make some change in their interpersonal functioning, such as ending isolation, since the distress experienced due to depression has usually become more intolerable than any interpersonal risks that they might take during group therapy sessions. The IDE may be used to ask this group member, for example, to observe how others in the group responded when he or she revealed the fear of disclosing feelings.

UNDERSTANDING YOUR INTERPERSONAL PROBLEMS AND PROFILE ON THE INTERPERSONAL CIRCUMPLEX

Group-CBASP helps participants gain a better understanding of their interpersonal difficulties and behaviors by focusing on their interpersonal goals, whether these are related to their TH or whether they are specific to one interpersonal interaction. They are encouraged to see that some form of intention or goal motivates most of our interpersonal interactions, whether it is conscious or not (Horowitz, 2004; Horowitz et al., 2006). Using the revised interpersonal model described by Horowitz et al. (2006), the group discusses the central role of one's interpersonal intentions or goals within each interpersonal *slice of time*," as described in the CBASP model, with a focus on how ambiguous goals may lead to miscommunication and to a frustrating or unsatisfying interpersonal outcome (Horowitz, 2004; Horowitz et al., 2006).

The DO, in a SA, is an interpersonal goal that can help reframe a depressed person's inner conflict into a person by environment interaction situated within the two dimensions of the Interpersonal Circumplex. An example of this is an

Interpersonal Domain (intimacy, self-disclosure, admitting errors, expressing negative emotions) that is difficult for a person to show others. The interpersonal space of the circumplex allows us to place the TH onto the two dimensions of Agency and Affiliation according to whether the person seeks to push others away, to please others in order to be liked, or any other behavior that may serve self-protective purposes. If a person avoids intimacy, then they may be situated on the Distant end of the Affiliation dimension. If a person tends to avoid expressing negative emotions, they may be situated on the lower right hand octant of the circumplex describing an overly accommodating style.

Some other examples of THs include interpersonal problems related to fear of being disliked by others, to fear of being judged, or to feelings of worthlessness or inadequacy. The behaviors displayed by individuals experiencing these problems, such as becoming overly critical or being socially avoidant, can be situated on the Interpersonal Circumplex, top left octant for the critical person and lower left octant for the avoidant one, along with the impact they may have on others.

Patients learn to observe how their self-protective behaviors to avoid fear can themselves become a "Desired" Outcome or goal that takes precedence in a particular "*slice of time*" over other more adaptive behaviors that would respond more accurately and effectively to the current situation and get them what they truly want. These self-protective behaviors may have an unintended impact on others because of the complementary reactions elicited, such as, for example, pushing others away. This realization often empowers group members to take more responsibility for the consequences of their behaviors on others, as they come to reflect on whether maladaptive behaviors they have learned agree with their values and with how they want to live their life. Through this process of discussion and exchange with others in the group, depressed patients develop mentalizing skills needed to improve their social functioning.

Group members use SAs to discuss their:

1. interpersonal motives (DOs);
2. interpersonal efficacy (Locke & Sadler, 2007), that is, their confidence in being able to reach these goals using an Action Interpretation;
3. behavioral strategies or Action Interpretations used to achieve a DO (outlined in the SA); and
4. coping strategy (adaptive or maladaptive) or emotional reactions when these efforts fail. These include continued avoidance or self-destructive behaviors versus reaching out for help and using problem-solving strategies.

During group therapy, members learn to self-administer the SA while paying attention to their central goal and then to appropriate behaviors and Action Interpretations needed to reach this goal. In doing so, they inevitably develop self-efficacy. They expand their repertoire of adaptive coping skills through trial and error and through active discussions in group therapy.

The adaptation of Horowitz et al.'s (2006) model to Group-CBASP facilitates a discussion involving all group members regarding the interpersonal profile of each person along with their adaptive or maladaptive behaviors and thoughts. By becoming more sensitized to their own miscommunications that result from ambiguous or unattainable DOs, members gain an understanding of why they often feel frustrated in their interpersonal relations. This has the effect of consolidating cohesion within the group and countering the defeatist and global thinking of persistent depression.

The four elements of the interpersonal profile discussed above are depicted in the four-piece diagram illustrated below (**Handout 16**). These four parts reflect the adaptation of Horowitz's interpersonal model to include the Action Interpretation, which reinforces interpersonal efficacy and enables learning of adaptive behaviors to reach desired interpersonal goals. Feeling confident about one's ability to act in an interpersonal situation has been shown in our research to increase the likelihood that depressed individuals will engage in these adaptive behaviors (Locke et al., 2015 submitted for publication).

The patient's workbook describes the interpersonal model in such a way that provides an introduction to the important concepts that can then be further elaborated within group discussions.

HANDOUT 16

YOUR INTERPERSONAL PROFILE:
HOW CAN IT HELP GET WHAT YOU WANT?

WHAT YOU WANT: THESE ARE YOUR GOALS

EFFICACY IS: HOW CONFIDENT YOU FEEL TO GET WHAT YOU WANT

WHAT BEHAVIORS DO YOU USE TO REACH YOUR GOALS? YOUR SOCIAL DOMAIN OR OTHER ADAPTIVE BEHAVIORS

HOW DO YOU COPE WHEN YOU DON'T GET WHAT YOU WANT INTERPERSONALLY?

Locke, 2000; Locke & Sadler, 2007; Horowitz et al., 2006

EXAMPLES OF CONTINGENT PERSONAL RESPONSIVITY (CPR) IN GROUP-CBASP

Group members will often spontaneously intervene from a friendly or friendly submissive stance toward others' hostile submissive behaviors in session. When this happens, the group therapist needs to intervene in a disciplined way to point out the effect that each has on the other. The following example demonstrates the use of CPR in Group-CBASP where the therapist intervened in a disciplined way to include a silent member and to respond to her dismissive comments when others expressed supportive behavior.

Case Example 1

Tina, a group member (62 years of age), is a woman who remained quiet throughout the group session, as she felt uncomfortable that day regarding a big decision she had recently made to purchase a car. She had previously consulted her son regarding another car she wanted to purchase and had followed his advice to wait and lived to regret this decision, feeling that she wanted to be more independent. She acknowledged having difficulty making such important decisions and had previously shared with the group her deep ambivalence about wanting on one hand to be autonomous and make her own decisions, without the intervention of her son, while on the other hand having serious doubts about whether the decision she did make to purchase the car was a result of a manic phase of her illness or whether she had even made the right decision. Several group members had previously reassured her, confirming the therapist's perception, that she had not been behaving in a manic way in the past several weeks and in fact did not have any other behavioral signs of mania; however, she remained skeptical about their friendly support. The day of the group session, this patient did not participate in the discussion regarding another member's SA. Her TH was related to fear of expressing negative emotions to others as others may discredit and reject her. In an attempt to include her in the conversation, the group therapist said:

THERAPIST: Tina we haven't heard your feedback about Jack's situation.
TINA: Yes . . . , I know. I haven't said much because I'm preoccupied today, as I had told you earlier *(at the beginning of the session Tina had approached the therapist to inform her of her discomfort that day)*.
THERAPIST: That's right; you did tell me but not the others in the group.
TINA: *(as she looked at group members looking back at her and waiting silently, Tina answered repeating what she had said in a previous session)* It's about the car I bought a couple of weeks ago again. I wonder if I made the right decision. I think I might have been in a manic state and I feel terrible about having acted so impulsively.

A discussion followed with group members attempting to reassure Tina that she appeared happy about her new car the first week that she purchased it. Tina, however, remained doubtful and wondered again if she had not acted impulsively. She repeated again that she realizes the good deal she made with this car but thought that she ought to have spoken to her son first. Group members appeared to be at a loss for what to say, having already discussed with her the fact that she had previously regretted speaking to her son about another car and following his advice. Then Bob, sitting right across from Tina, looked right at her with a kind smile and responded reassuringly:

BOB: Tina, you gave the matter some careful consideration and thought and spoke about your decision with us before making this purchase. I think you gave it enough consideration and I don't think you acted impulsively. You wanted to make this decision on your own and you did. It's normal to have some doubts about such a big expenditure, it happens to me as well.

Other group members followed Bob's example and supported Tina saying that she did not appear manic now nor before. Then Tina responded with irritation, saying:

TINA: You see, I didn't want to bore everyone with my troubles, it's no good anyway, no matter what I do, I can't get it right! Yes I know that I have little confidence in myself. I make a decision and then regret it.

No one knew what to say to Tina at that point. The group discussion may easily have continued to develop and move away from how Tina responded to the group if the group therapist had not intervened to underline the impact that Tina had on Bob and on others with her reply.

THERAPIST: Can we go back to the exchange between Tina and Bob please? Tina you said you didn't want to bore others with your troubles, then how do you explain Bob's response to you? When he spoke with you, how would you describe his behavior?

TINA: Well, he was very attentive and very kind to remember what I had previously said about this purchase to the group.

THERAPIST: Bob, or others in the group, how do you feel hearing Tina say that she doesn't want to bore you with her troubles?

BOB: I wasn't bored Tina, why would you say that? I understand how you feel. It happens to me too; I have difficulty making decisions and my wife usually ends up deciding for me and then I feel angry.

THERAPIST: You seem surprised Bob that Tina would think that she is boring you?

BOB: Yes I am.

THERAPIST: *(Therapist looks at Tina and holds back from acting as referee between Tina and Bob but rather waits for Tina to respond to Bob)*

TINA: I'm sorry Bob; I didn't think that my story would be of any interest to anyone.

MARIE: *(another group member)* I wasn't bored either Tina, we are here to support each other.

BOB: That's right and I appreciate being able to speak about my difficulties to you all as well.

THERAPIST: *(speaking to Bob, Marie, and the other group members)* So when Tina responds to your feedback to her, by saying that her story is not of interest to anyone, how do you feel? *(Therapist may model Disciplined Involvement at that point if no one else speaks)* I would feel like the carpet has been pulled from right under my feet! I noticed that the group only stopped giving you supportive comments Tina when you said that you didn't want to bore everyone. What impact do you think your comment may have had on the group?

TINA: Well, it seemed that I was boring them since they had nothing more to say.

THERAPIST: Yet, Bob or Marie what did you just say to Tina?

BOB: I said I wasn't bored, you remind me of myself.

THERAPIST: Tina, what do you hear?

TINA: He's not bored. He says he's like me.

THERAPIST: Then Tina why would you say to Bob and the others that your story is of no interest to them? At that point you seemed to pull the carpet from under this discussion that has been helpful to others.

TINA: I didn't even notice I had done that. You know I do this all the time and I never thought this would have an effect on people.

THERAPIST: That reminds me Tina that your Interpersonal Domain is about feeling that others will find you not credible or will reject you if you express your negative feelings. How has this played itself out right here in our discussion?

TINA: It hasn't! Everyone is very supportive; I just am not very receptive I guess.

THERAPIST: This is an opportunity for us to look at how our behaviors have an effect on each other and to think about the effect you want to have on others.

Comment

The group therapist is attentive to opportunities to point out, or choreograph, a response that underlines the consequences of interpersonal behaviors on others in the group. In this situation, the group therapist was attentive to one group member's silence, which is seen in CBASP as a manifestation of hostile submissive behavior, particularly coming from a group member who has been outspoken in the group before. The group therapist models active involvement in the group and this is what group members are encouraged to do throughout the duration of the group. Just as in individual therapy, the group therapist must remain cautious of not taking over the group discussion since group members often abdicate to the group therapist and avoid taking responsibility for group interactions.

Further discussions with Tina revealed that she had been withdrawing from others in her life after her husband's suicide which triggered her depression a few years ago. She reported feeling guilty about conflicts in the relationship she had with her husband and stated that she used to express many negative emotions to him, particularly anger. This guilt may have prevented her from completing the mourning process, as she explained that she deprived herself from experiencing pleasure or from expressing negative emotions as a form of self-punishment. She adopted a more hostile-submissive position in her relationships to avoid rejection, although the impact kept others at a distance. The group experience helped her realize that she had been depriving herself of deeper involvement in relationships with others by adopting a more hostile submissive stance without assuming responsibility for the consequences. By realizing her impact of pushing others away, she was able to see how her interpersonal behaviors kept her isolated, lonely, and unfulfilled. With this new insight, she was better able to determine what she ultimately wanted in relationships and how to facilitate achievement of these goals.

Case Example 2

The following example demonstrates well how group members learn to identify a "hot spot" in each other's SAs that are related to each person's difficult Interpersonal Domain or TH. The therapist reinforces this interactive exchange with particular focus on the impact of group members on each other.

Sue, aged 57, shared an interpersonal situation in which she had spoken with her father over the phone to ask how her mother, who is suffering from Alzheimer's disease, was doing. The father mentioned that the mother was currently attending her day program for individuals with Alzheimer's disease but that it was costly. Sue mentioned that her mother was able to be with others who experienced similar difficulties at that day program. The father replied that they would continue the program for now. The slice of time ended at that point as they stopped talking about this topic and hung up the phone.

Sue felt worried that her father might put an end to the day program for her mother but she did not express this concern to her father. In fact her behavior during the phone conversation with her father did not reveal any clue whatsoever that she was concerned about her mother since her voice had been very calm and "ordinary," as she described it. Instead, her thoughts had to do with her TH and were not relevant to the exchange with her father. Her *Interpretations* at the second step of the SA included thoughts about her father finding her boring because of her concern that she doesn't have much to say and cannot hold a conversation with anyone. Consequently, she expressed very little to her father over the phone. Another thought she had was about having called her father too late in the day and being at fault for not having enough time to give her father some "good reasons" to keep her mother in the day program. Finally, Sue was also thinking that she might not find good reasons to give her father to convince him to keep her mother going to that program.

Another group member remarked to Sue that she appeared to be more focused on blaming herself for sounding "boring" to her father or blaming herself for having called too late and this related to her TH of feeling that if she makes a mistake, she will be seen as inadequate. This concern about making mistakes took such proportions for Sue that she already felt overwhelmed about calling her father back since she felt that she would not have any useful suggestions to make on her mother's behalf. Sue expressed to the group her recurring problem of not calling friends by phone because of thoughts that she does not know what to talk about. This problem is now better understood as being related to high expectations that Sue places on herself. She felt that she needed to identify several good reasons why her father should keep her mother in the program, or she would be inadequate.

Group members remarked to Sue that in all her concern about having made mistakes, she never expressed to her father what she felt, that is, worried that he might remove her mother from the program (*the interpersonal motive*) and Sue agreed fully with this observation. Group members also pointed out to Sue that she had already given her father a good reason to allow her mother to continue attending the program, which was to be with others who experience similar difficulties. Sue agreed that she had overlooked this fact. Using the Interpersonal Circumplex, the group discussed where Sue's behavior with her father can be placed along the two dimensions of Agency and Affiliation, most probably within the unagentic and uncommunal octants of the circumplex that describe a more yielding and submissive interpersonal position.

Sue agreed with this and expressed her feeling that she is indeed able to assert herself (*interpersonal efficacy*) with her father; however, she had been too preoccupied about not bringing good enough arguments to her father about why her mother ought to continue the program.

This concern about making mistakes was apparent in her passive and submissive behaviors (*behavioral strategies*) during the phone conversation with her father. Sue's behaviors were brought to her attention during the third step of the SA, which she herself described.

The consequence of Sue's passive interpersonal behaviors in such situations is that she would usually avoid calling her father, or calling anyone for that matter, out of fear of sounding boring or not making a useful contribution (*coping strategy or emotional reaction*). This maladaptive coping strategy of avoidance reinforced Sue's feeling that she is unable to obtain the "complementary" response from others (in this example from her father) that would fulfill or satisfy her motive (in this case to talk about keeping her mother in the program). Because of this, Sue is likely to develop feelings of frustration and powerlessness that contribute to global thinking and depressive thoughts that "nothing will ever change in my life."

When Sue realized that the high expectations she placed on herself about coming up with just the right arguments, about calling at just the right time, and about not sounding boring when speaking with her father, she could easily see that her primary motive, to express her concern to her father, was impeded by her more hidden motive which was to perform "perfectly," as related to her TH.

Once Sue was able to see that she wanted to move herself out of the submissive and unagentic position on the Interpersonal Circumplex, which did not accurately reflect her feeling of efficacy regarding her ability to speak to her father, she then said she felt more confident about calling her father back and simply telling him what she wanted to say.

The group was able to discuss how the underlying motive, which was to tell her father that she did not want him to remove her mother from the program, was overcome by Sue's hidden motive, which is to appear "perfect" and avoid making mistakes. The SA, when used in conjunction with the TH, enables the therapist and group members to uncover hidden motives that take on a prominent role in a person's interpersonal behaviors.

GROUP-CBASP: SESSIONS 15 & 16

Homework review:

1. What activities did you do this past week?
2. Did you bring in a copy of the Situational Analysis with a difficult situation to discuss?

Session outline:

- Putting it all together
- Using the Situational Analysis to understand what you want and to learn how to get it
- Your Interpersonal Profile

Homework: For next week, choose an interpersonal situation that you found difficult to manage. Try to complete the Situational Analysis as much as you can and bring it in for the next group. We will do the Remediation Phase together.

PUTTING IT ALL TOGETHER

Now participants may understand that choosing a DO that is under their control and that is realistic and attainable means that they are learning to express what they want from others. Learning about what they want and how to get it helps individuals feel competent and good about themselves. It is positive problem-solving behavior that will reconnect them with themselves and with others around them. Participants now come to feel that what they do matters, as they come to understand the impact of their behaviors on others.

Using adaptive coping skills are protective factors against depression.

Group members are encouraged to ask themselves:

- "Am I clear about my goal when I interact with someone?"
- "Am I getting what I want in my relationships with others?"
- "Is what I want, something that is under my control, that I can reach?"
- "How satisfied am I about exchanges I have with others?"

YOUR INTERPERSONAL PROFILE

"Putting together the pieces of your interpersonal profile begins with asking yourself about what is <u>important</u> for you." The therapist reinforces the DO as a goal that is very specific to each slice of interpersonal interaction. Patients feel empowered to know that they can choose a DO that is under their control and is attainable with the help of an Action Interpretation. Appropriate behaviors can be practiced and role-played until a person feels confident and effective and understands the impact of these behaviors on others. Using adaptive coping strategies to tolerate frustration from unmet interpersonal goals are also important life skills that are best learned in a group format such as Group-CBASP.

These are the four pieces of the interpersonal profile that were the focus of this group treatment:

- Your interpersonal values will help you decide what you want, what your GOALS are, according to what is important for you in your interactions with others.
- Choosing a DO that is under your control, using an Action Interpretation, will help increase your CONFIDENCE in your ability to get what you want.
- The BEHAVIORS you use need to be effective and adaptive in reaching your goals, that is, in having the impact you want to have on others. You might use behaviors that do not help you get what you want, that is, get your DO, and these may need to change. Also, the social domain that you have problems with might drive you to behave in ways that stop you from getting what you want. You may think that what you want is to keep others away but you now see that this has resulted in being alone and depressive symptoms have not gone away. For example, if it is more important for you to not appear weak, then instead of asking for help, you might try to complete a difficult task alone and not succeed. So asking for help, which is an appropriate DO under your control, would be replaced by another behavior aimed at protecting your pride or saving face or perhaps avoiding fear of rejection. Here you have two motives that are in conflict: needing some help and protecting yourself. If neither one is fulfilled to your satisfaction, then how would you tend to react?
- Your COPING strategies used when you don't get what you want, no matter what behaviors you use, may include extreme emotional reactions, intense anger, substance or alcohol abuse, or other self-destructive behaviors, even

suicidal thoughts. Many depressed individuals oversleep to avoid interpersonal situations altogether because they feel frustrated about not getting what they want in interactions with others. Learning adaptive ways to cope, like the problem-solving SA, will help you solve one problem at a time and avoid defeatist thinking that leads to maladaptive behaviors.

Understanding how your interpersonal profile can work best to help you get what you want, reach your goals, and feel in control of your life is a very effective way to avoid relapses in depression.

GROUP-CBASP: SESSIONS 17 TO 20

Homework review:

1. What activities did you do this past week?
2. Did you bring in a copy of the Situational Analysis with a difficult situation to discuss?

Session outline:

*   Prepare for termination

    *   Assessing learning
    *   Reviewing your goals and saying good-bye

*   Group-CBASP maintenance and follow-up for relapse prevention
*   Ethical considerations for Group-CBASP

Homework: Keep using the Situational Analysis as an effective problem-solving strategy for all interpersonal situations that you find difficult to manage.

TERMINATION

In summary, Group-CBASP is a comprehensive treatment model to treat persistent depression. Group-CBASP includes strategies to: (1) increase felt emotional safety of the patient in order to facilitate approach behaviors and engagement within the group; (2) help patients learn about the impact of withdrawal and avoidant behaviors that perpetuate disconnection from their environment; and (3) develop adaptive interpersonal problem-solving skills to set and work toward desired interpersonal outcomes that are realistic, under one's control, and that build confidence and self-efficacy.

The goals of Group-CBASP, identified earlier in the manual, are realized, first, when the cohesion within the group helps to transform participants' pervasive interpersonal fears into an experience of interpersonal safety that allows each person to explore their own maladaptive interpersonal styles and accept feedback and support from others. The second goal is reached when participants change their avoidance behaviors within the group and learn to communicate with each other about what they want and feel in interpersonal situations and think about how they will reach their own desired interpersonal goals. Group members develop *perceived functionality*, previously described, by working all together on each other's SAs and gaining a better understanding of how others behave and the impact of these behaviors on themselves and on others.

Toward the end of Group-CBASP, members may review their behavioral activation logs, if they have completed them throughout the group, and observe how the challenges they have given themselves need to be incorporated into a new lifestyle that is more active and pleasurable. The emphasis is placed on practicing the skills learned, whether regarding a physical activity program, or regarding leisure activities, or regarding exposure to interpersonal situations that involve some risk-taking behaviors.

The SA is presented as an exercise to develop mentalizing and executive functions of participants whose cognitive functioning has been greatly compromised by chronic depression. Participants are encouraged to continue using the SA and to practice setting and working toward desired goals that are realistic and under their control, using adaptive behaviors. Follow-up Group-CBASP sessions may help reinforce generalization of learning.

Participants in Group-CBASP learn throughout their group experience about the impact of their behaviors on others within the group and can now make choices about whether this impact agrees with their values. The Interpersonal Circumplex provides a visual representation of the impact of their behaviors on others and this helps orient the patient toward the changes they want to make.

In the last two sessions of Group-CBASP, the group therapist asks participants to reflect on the objectives each person had at the beginning of the group, particularly regarding the TH and the one behavior they had identified to change. Now, after 18 weeks of group therapy, participants are better able to speak about their objectives moving forward. They usually speak about the impact of their interactions within the group and often comment about the group process. Participants will usually meet with an individual therapist at the end of Group-CBASP to discuss any follow-up needed and to explore the person's goals in more detail.

Saying good-bye is often difficult for many patients with persistent depression who have come to feel more connected to group members than they have felt for a long time. It is very important to address this issue of loss for some, separation for others, good-byes for others, in a manner that is best suited to the needs of individuals in each group. The decision to meet as a group outside of the clinic after the end of the 20-week group treatment is left up to the members and is not the therapist's responsibility. In fact, we would recommend that the therapist not participate in such informal meetings but instead offer monthly follow-up sessions and remain "disciplined" in his or her involvement.

GROUP-CBASP MAINTENANCE AND FOLLOW-UP FOR RELAPSE PREVENTION

Planned maintenance CBASP sessions within a group or individual format may be beneficial after group treatment is ended. Klein et al. (2004) provide preliminary evidence of the benefits of continuation and maintenance CBASP for persistent forms of depression. Klein et al. (2004) examined the efficacy of CBASP as a maintenance treatment for chronic forms of Major Depressive Disorder (MDD). Eighty-two patients who had responded to acute and continuation phase CBASP were randomized to monthly CBASP or assessment only for one year. Significantly fewer patients in the CBASP than assessment-only condition experienced a recurrence during the time of the study. The two conditions also differed significantly on change in depressive symptoms over time. Patients receiving assessment only experienced a small increase in symptoms over time, whereas patients receiving CBASP exhibited a small reduction in symptoms over time. The effect suggests that the benefits of maintenance CBASP may go beyond recurrence prevention and include continued (albeit slight) reduction of sub-threshold symptoms.

Overall, it is recommended that the use of CBASP, either in a group or individual format, as a maintenance treatment for chronic forms of MDD be implemented monthly for at least one year following the end of group therapy. A relapse prevention protocol designed to suit each patient's needs, implementing monthly individual or group CBASP sessions for one year post remission of depressive symptoms or after the allotted number of individual or group sessions, is also recommended if feasible. Relapse prevention may focus more on risk factors that were not addressed during Group-CBASP, such as reintegration back to work, adherence to medication and to a behavioral activation program, or reinforcing behavioral skills acquisition, all making use of SAs to focus on DOs.

ETHICAL CONSIDERATIONS FOR GROUP-CBASP

Persistent depression is a complex disorder often associated with early-onset, early-trauma, co-morbid conditions such as personality disorders, psychiatric or medical conditions, or with an unstable or chaotic lifestyle. The importance of a continued re-evaluation of the initial diagnosis to address any other emerging difficulties cannot be emphasized enough. In fact, the best treatment approach offered to these patients is one carried out in a team where the pharmacological and medical follow-ups are maintained and other resources are mobilized to help the patient reintegrate back into his or her community. As such, the group therapist needs to consider the appropriateness of referrals to other health professionals following the end of Group-CBASP and this is best discussed with patients in individual sessions at the end of Group-CBASP. Patients are encouraged to pursue the process of recovery by identifying the suitable next step in their trajectory.

PART

IV

ASSESSING CHANGE IN GROUP-CBASP

MEASURING SKILLS ACQUISITION IN GROUP-CBASP

Individuals experiencing persistent depression accept to join a predominantly group-oriented treatment modality because they agree to break their isolation by engaging with others in a group setting and they agree that something needs to change in their interpersonal relations to make them feel more effective and satisfied with themselves and others. These distressed patients often cannot identify on their own what needs to change in their interpersonal interactions and may even have difficulty noticing when change does take place. It is very helpful to underline change mechanisms for these patients and to help them navigate through the quagmire of their interpersonal difficulties.

For the group experience to become rewarding, the therapist needs to help these patients, who often feel overwhelmed by negative global thinking, focus on the "one important maladaptive interpersonal behavior that they need to change that will overthrow their chronic depression" (personal communication, McCullough 2014). This helps make the group experience rewarding and emphasizes the role of positive reinforcement obtained from healthy interactions between group members. In addition, group participants experience relief from the hopelessness and despair perpetuated by their long-standing social isolation. Indeed, resolving interpersonal problems together in the group, using SAs, enables participants to develop interpersonal efficacy and competency. Measuring change in the acquisition of interpersonal efficacy is a very powerful tool to demonstrate the effects of empowerment and its impact on one's life.

The Self-Administered Interpersonal Discrimination Exercise (IDE)

The first goal of Group-CBASP, cited earlier as being the patient's capacity to discriminate between negative reactions from significant others and the more appropriate and supportive reactions from group members (thus increasing *felt emotional safety*), is measured directly using a form developed by McCullough et al. (2010) to score the learning acquired in the IDE. This form, called the Self-Administered Interpersonal Discrimination Exercise (Sad-IDE, **Form 7 in**

Appendix), can be completed by the patient to outline the difference between anticipated negative reactions that patients received from significant others and the actual reactions obtained from group members to their current interpersonal behaviors.

This exercise is done within the group when a participant exhibits a behavior that is characteristic of the Interpersonal Domain of difficulty identified in the individual sessions prior to group therapy. That is, when a patient discloses or makes a mistake or any other behavior typical of the four interpersonal domains, the therapist highlights this behavior and asks group members to indicate their reaction to the patient's behavior. The therapist keeps the discussion focused on the patient's risk-taking behavior in the group and then the patient is asked to think about how the significant other who had adversely influenced the patient would have responded to such behavior exhibited, or was expected to respond to the patient, in a way that promoted maladaptive learning and inhibited personal growth. The patient is then asked to describe the group members' reactions to him or her while exhibiting that behavior and is encouraged to describe the difference between the significant other's reaction and the group members' reactions. The patient will then be in a position to complete the Sad-IDE with direct feedback from group members. The therapist collects these forms to analyse change realized for each group member.

The Personal Questionnaire (PQ)

Another method can be used to assess a patient's capacity to recognize the consequences of his or her interpersonal behaviors on others and the changes in maladaptive learning acquired with a significant other. This method, recommended by McCullough (2006, pp. 163–167; et al. 2010), also makes use of the TH established at the initial individual sessions and is called the *Personal Questionnaire* (PQ). The PQ was developed by Shapiro (McCullough & Kasnetz, 1982; Shapiro, 1961; Shapiro, Litman, Nias, & Hendry, 1973) as a *patient self-report methodology* to help patients observe themselves moving toward change in their interpersonal behaviors. The PQ is a paired-comparison technique using three cards containing a formulation of the TH that is worded in a way representing *illness-level functioning* (card 1) at baseline; *improvement-level functioning* (card 2) during group therapy; and *recovery-level functioning* (card 3) also during group therapy. An example of the formulation follows:

Card 1—*Illness level*: *More often than not* I feel that if I disclose my feelings and needs to others in the group, then they will see that I am weak and silly and will dislike me.
Card 2—*Improvement*: *Sometimes* I feel that if I disclose my feelings and needs to others in the group, then this will not be seen as weakness; it is OK to say what I feel.
Card 3—*Recovery*: *More often than not* I feel that if I disclose my feelings and needs to others in the group, then this will not be seen as weakness; it is OK to say what I feel.

Each group member has a set of three cards with their own TH outlined in each card, as shown above. The improvement-level functioning in card two and recovery-level in card three are developed at the same time as the TH. Each patient is then asked to monitor his or her own learning throughout treatment by comparing each card with the other in a paired comparison rating task done every three weeks. The therapist records the choices made by each patient on a form and this exercise can also provide an opportunity to discuss the learning acquired in group therapy with regards to the TH. The reader is referred to McCullough's reference for a discussion of the administration and scoring of the PQ. Therapists may decide to ask patients to rate on a scale from one to ten the degree to which they adhere to each phrase, as an alternative to the scoring procedure developed by Shapiro et al. (1973).

With regards to whether the therapist ought to see the patient's ratings or not will depend on whether this exercise is used for research purposes or whether the therapist would like to incorporate it as a method of reinforcing learning acquired throughout Group-CBASP. The current authors have used the PQ exercise as part of group discussions allowing group members to witness each other's progress or difficulties. The beneficial impact of disclosing the patients' ratings within the group, thus generating therapeutic discussions about interpersonal reciprocity, far outweighs the idea of having blind raters do the exercise with group members outside of the group context.

The Patient Performance Rating Form (PPRF)

The second goal of Group-CBASP also concerns the patient's ability to recognize the impact of his or her interpersonal behaviors on others with the added component of achieving *perceived functionality*, defined as the ability to reach Desired Outcomes in interpersonal situations. Learning to obtain a satisfactory Desired Outcome and understanding how and why this goal is achieved are the goals of the SA. The SA is a technique practiced throughout Group-CBASP to enable participants to become autonomous at identifying the consequences of their interpersonal behaviors and the outcomes they would like to obtain that are within their control and which the environment can produce.

Rating the patient's acquisition of learning using the SA is done with an instrument called the *Patient Performance Rating Form* (PPRF) (Manber et al., 2003; McCullough, 2000). This instrument has been shown to have good interrater reliability in a large multi-cite study of CBASP's effectiveness (Manber et al., 2003). Criterion performance is described as the patient's ability to successfully administer the five-step SA procedure twice in succession while receiving a score of one for correctness and zero for incorrectness, obtaining a total score of up to five points for the entire five-step SA exercise. The entire PPRF procedure and rating form are described in **Form 8** in the Appendix.

In Group-CBASP, the therapist can collect all the SAs completed by participants doing the exercises together in the group, as described in sessions 3 and 4. This allows for the evaluation of learning acquired throughout group therapy for each participant.

ASSESSING INTERPERSONAL DISPOSITIONS IN PERSISTENT DEPRESSION

Group-CBASP also lends itself well to an exploration of interpersonal impacts or interpersonal complementarity using the Interpersonal Circumplex. The use of the Impact Message Inventory (IMI: Kiesler & Schmidt, 1993) is recommended by McCullough (2000) as a means for the individual therapist to determine the impact or stimulus value that the patient is likely to have on him or her throughout therapy. The IMI is a self-report measure typically completed by a person regarding his or her covert reactions (emotional, cognitive, or behavioral) that are "pulled" or "invited" by another person's behaviors. McCullough suggests that the therapist completes the IMI early in treatment, after the TH has been established for a particular patient. The IMI helps the therapist identify his or her own most likely stimulus value or impact that he or she will have on each patient within the group. Therapists rate patients, on a scale from one (not at all) to four (very much), on seven impact items within each of eight interpersonal octants: Dominant, Hostile-Dominant, Hostile, Hostile-Submissive, Submissive, Friendly Submissive, Friendly, and Friendly Dominant.

The 56–item inventory is scored by obtaining a mean impact score for each octant. The therapist will be able to map his responses onto the Interpersonal Circumplex comprised of two underlying independent dimensions of Affiliation or Agency. These are considered two higher-order motives along the hierarchy of needs (Horowitz, 2004). When the IMI was constructed the two dimensions were labeled Affiliation (ranging from Hostile to Friendly) and Dominance (ranging from Dominant to Submissive). The Dominant scale items are likely to evoke feelings within the therapist of being "bossed around" by the patient, whereas the Submissive scale is likely to evoke feelings within the therapist of being "in charge." The therapist uses this information to monitor his or her reaction in order to avoid the pitfalls of responding inappropriately in frustration or anger toward a persistently depressed patient whose primary interpersonal stance is submissive or passive-aggressive.

The pull on the therapist to adopt a hostile dominant or dominant role, complementary to the tendency of the predominant group dynamic to be rather submissive and/or hostile submissive, is particularly strong in group therapy with severely or persistently depressed patients. Instead, the group therapist needs to remain in a friendly or friendly dominant role and may sometimes respond from a friendly submissive position in order to promote the initiative of other group members who become friendly dominant.

McCullough's tenets regarding the interpersonal hostile-submissive position of persistently depressed patients were confirmed in a study comparing chronically depressed patients from a 12-site (N=681) comparative clinical trial (Keller et al., 2000) to a nonclinical, normative comparison group and to an acutely depressed clinical comparison group. Persistently depressed patients present with more hostile and hostile-dominant and lower friendly and friendly dominant impacts on their therapists than acutely depressed patients' impacts on their therapists or a normative comparison groups' impacts on a rating other (Constantino et al., 2008). Furthermore, by the end of treatment, the persistently depressed patients' impact messages were mostly equivalent with those of the two comparison groups (being more friendly, friendly dominant, and friendly submissive) except for the friendly dominant impacts which continued to be lower for the persistently depressed patients compared to the normative sample.

Decreases in hostile submissive impacts among persistently depressed patients were also found to be associated with greater reductions in depressive symptoms over time and with a positive response to treatment. However, increases in friendly dominant impact messages over the course of treatment did not predict improvement in depression or treatment response (Constantino et al., 2012). Indeed, it appears that decreases in hostile submissiveness may reflect changes along the dimension of Affiliation which in turn may pull for more friendliness on the part of the therapist that is picked up with the IMI, whereas changes in levels of dominance or assertiveness may have less of an interpersonal impact (Constantino et al., 2012). Further evidence confirms that impact messages of depressed patients reveal a more submissive interpersonal style than for patients with other psychiatric diagnoses (Grosse Holtforth et al., 2012).

Grosse Holtforth et al. (2012) also found that over the course of psychotherapy, depressed patients decreased on the three submissive and the hostile circumplex octants and became more dominant and friendly dominant, respectively. The decrease of submissive and hostile submissive styles was associated with positive outcomes, whereas the change in friendly submissiveness was again unrelated to outcomes. Contrary to the findings of Constantino et al. (2008) whose sample had impact messages primarily within the hostile or hostile-submissive octants, Grosse Holtforth et al. (2012) report a heterogeneity in impact messages of depressed patients that correspond to the four octants of the Interpersonal Circumplex, although almost half of the depressed patients were in the friendly submissive cluster. The authors suggest that their sample of depressed patients may not correspond to the profile of persistent depression and this may in turn point to the increased finding of interpersonal pathoplasticity with Major Depressive Disorder (Cain et al., 2012).

Just as the IMI is a useful instrument to show the therapist how he or she may be "pulled" to respond to the depressed patient in an inappropriate way, other self-report instruments are also useful to provide the depressed patient with a personalized profile of interpersonal dispositions such as interpersonal values, interpersonal efficacy or competency, and interpersonal problems or distress experienced. The use of these self-report measures is by no means essential to the CBASP model, whether in individual or group therapy; although the use of the IMI to better understand the therapist's stimulus value with patients is important to consider using. The IMI may be given within the group to help members better understand the impact of their behaviors on others and generate more group discussion about the TH and their related Interpersonal Domain.

The first author administered the Circumplex Scale of Interpersonal Values (CSIV: Locke, 2000), the Circumplex Scale of Interpersonal Efficacy (CSIE: Locke & Sadler, 2007) and the Inventory of Interpersonal Problems (IIP; Horowitz et al., 2000) self-report measures as part of a battery of measures in a randomized controlled trial to assess the comparative effectiveness of Group-CBASP versus group Behavioral Activation, with results currently being analyzed. Locke (2000) developed the CSIV, which measures the value that individuals place on certain interpersonal outcomes or modes of conduct associated with each octant of the Interpersonal Circumplex. Respondents rate (on a scale from zero to four) the importance of various interpersonal outcomes or behaviors that might occur within the group setting. The scale demonstrates very good internal consistency for the eight scales of the circumplex, with Cronbach's alphas ranging from .76 to .86. The intercorrelations of the eight CSIV scales reveal the expected positive correlations between adjacent octants and high negative correlations between polar opposite octants on the Interpersonal Circumplex.

The CSIE measures individuals' confidence in their ability to successfully perform interpersonal behaviors associated with each of the eight octants of the Interpersonal Circumplex (such as giving orders or following orders). Respondents rate (on a scale from zero to ten) how confident or sure they are that they can do certain specific behaviors within the group setting. Higher scores indicate greater efficacy. The scales of the CSIE have been shown to have internal consistency (Cronbach alphas range from .66 to .83 for each of the eight scales). They conform to a circumplex structure and show good convergent validity with the scales of the IIP and CSIV.

There is evidence supporting the findings that both efficacy and values, as described above, have shared variance regarding the prediction of interpersonal behavior, although efficacy alone explains unique variance in interpersonal behavior that is not explained by values (Locke & Sadler, 2007). Locke and Sadler (2007) explain that this follows Bandura's (1997) hypothesis that "people will not attempt a behavior if they do not believe that they can complete it successfully."

Information for hand-scoring the CSIV and CSIE is provided in the Appendix (**Form 9**) along with norms for a non-psychiatric population (**Form 10**) that may be used as a general point of reference. The Interpersonal Circumplex for the CSIV and CSIE are also included in the Appendix (**Handouts 13 & 14**) and will be found in the text of the patient's workbook to help demonstrate the eight interpersonal dispositions for each measure. For further information on these measures as well as free copies to download of the 64-item CSIV, a shorter 32-item version of the CSIV, and the 32-item CSIE please refer to the website of the author who developed them, Dr. K. D. Locke at www.webpages.uidaho.edu/klocke/.

The IIP (Horowitz et al., 2000) is a 64-item self-report instrument that identifies a person's most salient interpersonal difficulties. A brief version containing 32 items (IIP-32) is used instead as it preserves the scale structure of the 64-item version and retains the four items of each scale with the highest item-total correlations. The internal consistency for the IIP-32 scale is high with reliability coefficients ranging from .68 to .93.

In a pilot study (Sayegh et al., 2012) of Group-CBASP with chronically depressed outpatients, conducted by the present authors, 12 sessions of group therapy showed significant decreases in self-reported symptoms of depression and in the use of Emotion-focused Coping (Endler & Parker, 1999), as well as increases in overall social adjustment (Weissman, 1999) and Interpersonal Efficacy (Locke & Sadler, 2007) when compared to their pre-treatment levels. Moreover, the beneficial effects on overall depression and adjustment were quite strong. Group-CBASP appeared to facilitate the acquisition of interpersonal skills as seen in patients' improved Interpersonal Efficacy in the area of agentic behaviors that include assertive, self-confident, and independent behaviors. The authors have since recommended extending the duration of Group-CBASP to 20 sessions in order for improvements to reach levels of remission for depression.

APPENDICES

FORM 1

DO YOU HAVE MAJOR DEPRESSION?

You may have what is called major depression if you have at least **five** of the symptoms discussed below during a period of **two weeks or more**. These symptoms must cause you significant distress or impairment in at least one important area of your life, like work or social functioning, so do not include them if they only bother you a little or you do not experience them daily.

You may have major depression if you feel **depressed or sad** or have a **lack of interest or pleasure** in things that you used to get pleasure from or were interested in. You must also have these symptoms **for most of the day nearly every day during at least two weeks** for this to be part of a diagnosis of major depression. Additionally, you **must have at least four of the following symptoms (or three, if you have both depressed mood/irritability and lack of interest or pleasure)** to make a determination that you have major depression. These additional symptoms that you may have include:

1. Significant changes in weight or appetite, such as weight loss even when you are not dieting or weight gain or decrease or increase in appetite nearly every day;
2. Problems with sleep, in the form of either sleeping too much or having problems falling or staying asleep almost every day;
3. Feeling either too agitated or too slowed down nearly every day;
4. Suffering from fatigue or excessive feelings of being tired almost every day;
5. Feeling worthless and/or having feelings of guilt and shame that are excessive for the situation;
6. Having difficulty thinking or concentrating such as having problems making decisions almost every day;
7. Having repeated thoughts about death or killing yourself or having a plan to kill yourself or having tried to kill yourself in the past.

If you have five of these symptoms (including at least one of the first two) and they have lasted for at least two weeks and cause you significant distress or interfere with your functioning daily, then you may have major depression and it is best that you consult your doctor about your symptoms.

FORM 2

DO YOU HAVE PERSISTENT DEPRESSIVE DISORDER (DYSTHYMIA)?

You may have what is called persistent depression or dysthymia if you have depressed or sad mood for most of the day nearly every day for at least **two years**. Also, during this same two-year period if you suffer from persistent depression you may have at least two of the following symptoms:

1. Increased or decreased appetite or eating behavior;
2. Difficulties either falling asleep and staying asleep or sleeping too much;
3. Having low energy or excessive fatigue;
4. Having low self-esteem;
5. Difficulty concentrating or making decisions; and/or
6. Feeling hopeless.

During the two-year period, you have probably never been without these symptoms for more than two months at a time. These symptoms cause a lot of distress and interfere with your ability to function socially, at work and in other important areas of your life. Persistent depression may take on a different course for each person:

1. **Dysthymia**: A mild to moderate depression, which lasts two or more years, usually beginning during adolescence.
2. **Double depression**: A single major depressive episode or recurrent major depression without recovery between episodes, on top of a dysthymia.
3. **Recurrent major depression**: This depression is called "major depression, recurrent, without full recovery between episodes and with no dysthymia." Some symptoms usually persist between episodes.
4. **Chronic major depression**: Full criteria for a major depressive episode with two or more years' duration.

If you recognize that you have the symptoms above and they have lasted for at least two years without any significant amount of time of feeling better, you may be suffering from persistent depression or what is also called dysthymia. This is a chronic and debilitating disorder and it is best that you consult your doctor about your symptoms. Group-CBASP is an effective psychotherapy designed to treat both major depression and persistent depression.

HANDOUT 2

MOOD CHART

You can use this Mood Chart to check your mood at the beginning or at the end of the day. Place a check (✓) in the box that best describes how you feel today. The top row of numbers is the days of the month. If you feel better, put a check in the boxes above the "0." If you feel worse, put a check in the boxes below the "0."

You can also record at the bottom of the page the number of hours of sleep you had each day and the minutes you spent doing an activity.

© 2016, *Group Workbook for Treatment of Persistent Depression: Cognitive Behavioral Analysis System of Psychotherapy (CBASP) Patient's Guide*, Liliane Sayegh & J. Kim Penberthy, Routledge

MOOD CHART

Fill in a square on the chart in the <u>morning</u> or <u>bedtime</u>:

Name: _____

How has your mood been today?

Month/Year: _____

DAY →		1	2	3	4	5	6	7	8	9	10	11	12	13	14	15	16	17	18	19	20	21	22	23	24	25	26	27	28	29	30	31
Extremely good all the time	+5																															
Feeling good almost all the time	+4																															
Feeling good most of the time	+3																															
Feeling good a lot of the time	+2																															
Feeling good more often than bad	+1																															
Not feeling good or bad particularly	0																															
Feeling bad more often than good	−1																															
Feeling bad a lot of the time	−2																															
Feeling bad most of the time	−3																															
Feeling bad almost all the time	−4																															
Extremely bad all the time	−5																															
Hours of sleep last 24 hours																																
Minutes of activities per day																																

FORM 3

CBASP SIGNIFICANT OTHER HISTORY

1st Significant Other: *(person's name)*

What was it like growing up/being around (   )?

How did (   ) influence the course of your life?

How did (   ) influence you to be the kind of person you are now?

STAMP:

2nd Significant Other: *(person's name)*

What was it like growing up/being around (   )?

How did (   ) influence the course of your life?

How did (   ) influence you to be the kind of person you are now?

STAMP:

3rd Significant Other: *(person's name)*

What was it like growing up/being around (   )?

How did (   ) influence the course of your life?

How did (   ) influence you to be the kind of person you are now?

STAMP:

Form 3 was inspired by Sarah Meshberg-Cohen, Ph.D. and used with permission from J.P. McCullough, Jr. (2000). *Treatment for Chronic Depression: Cognitive Behavioral Analysis System of Psychotherapy (CBASP).* New York: Guilford Press

FORM 3

4th Significant Other: *(person's name)*

What was it like growing up/being around (   )?

How did (   ) influence the course of your life?

How did (   ) influence you to be the kind of person you are now?

STAMP:

5th Significant Other: *(person's name)*

What was it like growing up/being around (   )?

How did (   ) influence the course of your life?

How did (   ) influence you to be the kind of person you are now?

STAMP:

6th Significant Other: *(person's name)*

What was it like growing up/being around (   )?

How did (   ) influence the course of your life?

How did (   ) influence you to be the kind of person you are now?

STAMP:

Form 3 was inspired by Sarah Meshberg-Cohen, Ph.D. and used with permission from J.P. McCullough, Jr. (2000). *Treatment for Chronic Depression: Cognitive Behavioral Analysis System of Psychotherapy (CBASP).* New York: Guilford Press

FORM 4

CBASP INTERPERSONAL QUESTIONNAIRE (CIQ)

Patient's Name: _____ (Please Print)

Date: _____

<u>Instructions</u>: Please read each statement carefully and *circle* one answer for each statement that best describes your feelings <u>right now</u>.

1. I'm worried about getting close to someone in a relationship because of what might happen to me.

   Not at all___   Somewhat ___   Neutral ___   Moderately___   Extremely___
      1   *2*   *3*   *4*   *5*

2. I'm concerned that if I disclose my personal concerns or needs with someone, they might reject me or think I'm being ridiculous.

   Not at all___   Somewhat ___   Neutral ___   Moderately___   Extremely___
      1   *2*   *3*   *4*   *5*

3. If I let someone know that I'm frustrated or angry with them, I fear they will reject me or not like me.

   Not at all___   Somewhat ___   Neutral ___   Moderately___   Extremely___
      1   *2*   *3*   *4*   *5*

4. I worry that if I let someone know what I really need or want, they'll think I'm weird or odd.

   Not at all___   Somewhat ___   Neutral ___   Moderately___   Extremely___
      1   *2*   *3*   *4*   *5*

5. If I make a mistake around someone, I really worry about what will happen to me.

   Not at all___   Somewhat ___   Neutral ___   Moderately___   Extremely___
      1   *2*   *3*   *4*   *5*

6. If I get close to someone, I'm afraid that I will make a fool of myself.

   Not at all___   Somewhat ___   Neutral ___   Moderately___   Extremely___
      1   *2*   *3*   *4*   *5*

7. I worry that if I express my frustration or irritation toward someone, they'll think I'm abnormal or strange or they'll get mad at me.

   Not at all___   Somewhat ___   Neutral ___   Moderately___   Extremely___
      1   *2*   *3*   *4*   *5*

8. If I share or disclose myself with someone, I'm afraid they may hurt me in some way.

   Not at all___   Somewhat ___   Neutral ___   Moderately___   Extremely___
      1   *2*   *3*   *4*   *5*

© J.P. McCullough, Jr. (2008). *CBASP Intensive Training Workbook*. Department of Psychology. Virginia Commonwealth University. Richmond, Virginia 23284–2018

FORM 4

9. I always feel that if I don't do what I'm told, I will make mistakes and then I'll be punished in some way.

    Not at all___   Somewhat ___   Neutral ___   Moderately___   Extremely___
        1   *2*   *3*   *4*   *5*

10. Others will think that I'm strange or weird if they really get to know me in a relationship.

    Not at all___   Somewhat ___   Neutral ___   Moderately___   Extremely___
        1   *2*   *3*   *4*   *5*

11. I cannot let anyone know that I'm upset, angry, or frustrated with them because they'll get upset or reject me.

    Not at all___   Somewhat ___   Neutral ___   Moderately___   Extremely___
        1   *2*   *3*   *4*   *5*

12. I feel that I must be perfect around others and not make mistakes or they'll think less of me.

    Not at all___   Somewhat ___   Neutral ___   Moderately___   Extremely___
        1   *2*   *3*   *4*   *5*

© J.P. McCullough, Jr. (2008). *CBASP Intensive Training Workbook*. Department of Psychology. Virginia Commonwealth University. Richmond, Virginia 23284–2018

100 APPENDICES

FORM 5

CBASP INTERPERSONAL QUESTIONNAIRE (CIQ)—
ADMINISTRATION AND SCORING

Session 2

PROCEDURE FOR USING THE *CIQ DURING SESION 2*

1. Administer Significant Other History (SOH)
2. Then, Administer the CIQ to the Patient

The answers to the CIQ may provide added support for your TH Domain decision derived from the SOH. The CIQ Domain attaining the *highest cumulative total score* should be closely related to the SOH TH domain you have selected.

Post-Session 2

Scoring Procedures for Psychotherapist:

Domain Key for Scoring:

Being Intimate/Getting Close with/to someone (a <u>relationship</u> implied): 1, 6, 10

Personal Disclosure of Oneself/Expression of Needs (a patient <u>behavior</u> implied): 2, 4, 8

Making Mistakes around Someone: 5, 9, 12

Expressing Negative Affect to Someone: 3, 7, 11

3. Add up the *total cumulative scores* in each Transference Domain to determine the domain with the highest score:

   Total Domain Scores:
   Intimacy _____
   Person Disclosure/Needs _____
   Making Mistakes _____
   Expressing Negative Affect _____

4. *Construct a TH using the SOH information and the Domain that attains the highest cumulative score:*

© J.P. McCullough, Jr. (2008). *CBASP Intensive Training Workbook.* Department of Psychology. Virginia Commonwealth University. Richmond, Virginia 23284–2018

FORM 6

CASE EXAMPLE OF ALICE

(modified from a real case)

Alice is a 45-year-old divorced mother living alone with her two children (aged 9 and 11). Her parents live close by and solicit her help very often. She left the father of her children due to psychological abuse on his part but was feeling guilty wondering if she made the right decision. She is an accountant and admits that she succeeded professionally to prove to her father that she could "be somebody." She is treated for a persistent depression that lasted for over three years. At the time that she began Group-CBASP she had not been working for almost two years and she now wonders if her father was right in saying to her that she would "not be able to do anything".

The following are the results of the SOH interview with Alice.

Alice named the significant people in her life in the following order: Mother, Father, brother Fred, ex-husband, ex-mother-in-law.

SOH

1st Significant Other: Mother
What was it like growing up/being around your mother?
She was always sick, never played, wasn't able to do things. It was hard for me to see her sick. I did a lot of chores, it was work for me. I grew up fast. She was physically affectionate, we cooked together.
How did your mother influence the course of your life?
Part of me is stuck in childhood. I didn't grow up properly. She was submissive and didn't fight back.
How did your mother influence you to be the kind of person you are now?
STAMP: I was submissive to my ex-husband and we did whatever he wanted.

2nd Significant Other: Father
What was it like growing up/being around your father?
He was tough, he put us down a lot, often said "You won't be able to do anything" to me mostly, not my brother. I feel that way now and I don't know if I can raise my children by myself. He's angry with me for having left my husband. He wasn't affectionate, I was afraid of him. He bullied my mother physically and bullied us verbally. He was an alcoholic.
How did your father influence the course of your life?
Women are supposed to be oppressed or they're less than a man.

How did your father influence you to be the kind of person you are now?

I became an accountant to show him that a woman could succeed.

STAMP: I feel beat-up, not good enough.

3rd Significant Other: <u>Older Brother</u>

What was it like growing up/being around your brother?

We didn't play together; he's six years older than me. He had his friends. Then when our mother became ill we teamed up to help her. He took charge and told me what to do.

How did your brother influence the course of your life?

He's also an accountant and I followed his example. He is smart, gets what he wants, and knows what he wants. I wanted him to recognize me.

How did your brother influence you to be the kind of person you are now?

He still tells me what to do.

STAMP: I look up to him, he knows what to do.

4th Significant Other: <u>Ex-Husband</u>

What was it like being around your ex-husband?

We were together 14 years. In the beginning he decided everything we would do and where we would go. If he picked a fight, it was always my fault and I didn't defend myself. He was controlling!

How did your ex-husband influence the course of your life?

He set everything up for me and I was content to follow.

How did your ex-husband influence you to be the kind of person you are now?

STAMP: I became co-dependent, can't manage on my own.

5th Significant Other: <u>Ex-mother-in-law</u>

What was it like being around your ex-mother-in-law?

She did things for me, took care of the kids, made meals, she took charge. She was affectionate but she excused my ex-husband's hostile behavior, even his death threats to me.

> **How did your ex-mother-in-law influence the course of your life?**
>
> She enabled the abuse to go on and my co-dependency because whenever I asked her for help, she did help.
>
> ---
>
> **How did your ex-mother-in-law influence you to be the kind of person you are now?**
>
> ---
>
> **STAMP: I'm submissive and co-dependent as she was with her husband.**

The results obtained by Alice on the Interpersonal Questionnaire revealed high scores on all four Interpersonal Domains. However, for Alice, expressing negative emotions was something she was not able to do because she feared the consequences. Following her experiences with significant others, she learned that she must go along with what she is told to do and be grateful. This was reinforced by her extensive self-doubt regarding her capabilities as a mother. Although she decided to leave her husband, she also feels very unable to cope on her own.

In light of her fear of disappointing others, Alice agreed with her therapist's assessment that expressing negative emotions to others raised her fear about being rejected. The TH constructed with Alice, relative to how she would interact with others in the group, was the following:

> *"If I express negative feelings, particularly anger, then others will judge me negatively; they'll think I'm not good enough."*

The phrase that represented one change that Alice wanted to make was to allow herself to express her anger and tell herself that she is "good enough," as such.

During Group-CBASP, Alice learned about her interpersonal profile, depicted in the three circumplex graphs below. The solid lines indicate her reported interpersonal problems, values, and efficacy before the group began and the dashed lines indicate the same interpersonal dispositions after 20 weeks of Group-CBASP. The Interpersonal Problems reported by Alice centered on feeling socially inhibited, avoidant, unassertive, and unable to speak with authority. She confirms that she tried to compensate for feeling ineffective by being too giving, self-sacrificing, placing other people's needs before her own. By the end of Group-CBASP, Alice had learned:

> *"I need to be honest with myself and with what **I** want. I need to be able to express myself calmly, firmly and assertively and say what my wants are. I need to have expectations of others. I must keep in mind that I do not control what others feel and want."*

Her scores on the Interpersonal Circle of Problems reflect the change in feeling less avoidant of others, less unassertive, and less self-sacrificing. Regarding the Interpersonal Circles of Values, Alice learned that she attributes value and importance to expressing herself openly, to feeling connected to others, and attributes less importance to being defensively avoidant or hostile. Regarding the Interpersonal Circle of Self-Efficacy, Alice has gained confidence in her ability to be assertive as well as help others but also express anger when needed.

Alice's scores on measures of depressive symptoms, coping strategies, and changes in the TH (using the PQ described above) were assessed before group began (Time 1), ten weeks after the group started (Time 2), at the end of the group (Time 3), and three months after the end of Group-CBASP (Time 4). The PQ was assessed every third session from the start to the end of group therapy. The results are depicted below.

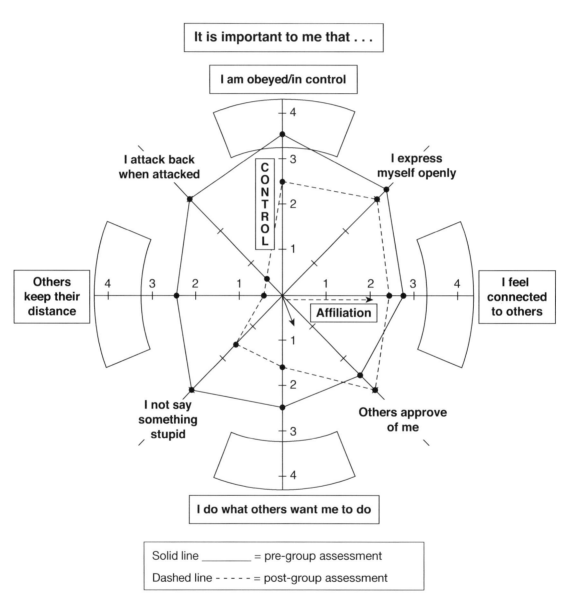

Your Interpersonal Circumplex—Values

Locke (2000)

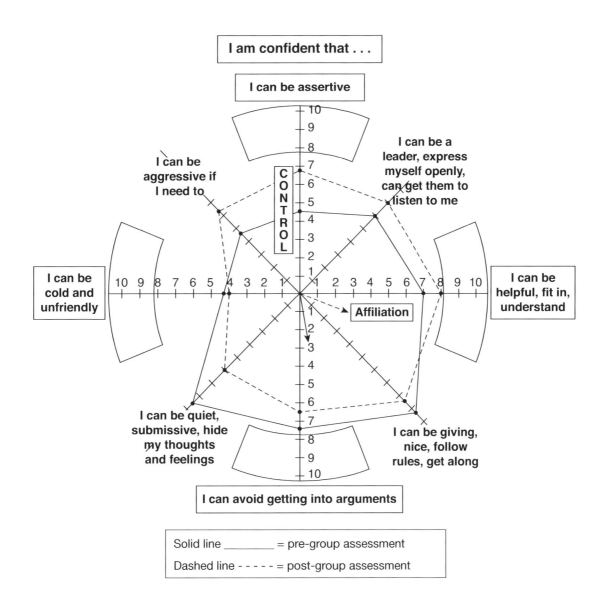

Your Interpersonal Circumplex—Self-Efficacy

Locke and Sandler (2007)

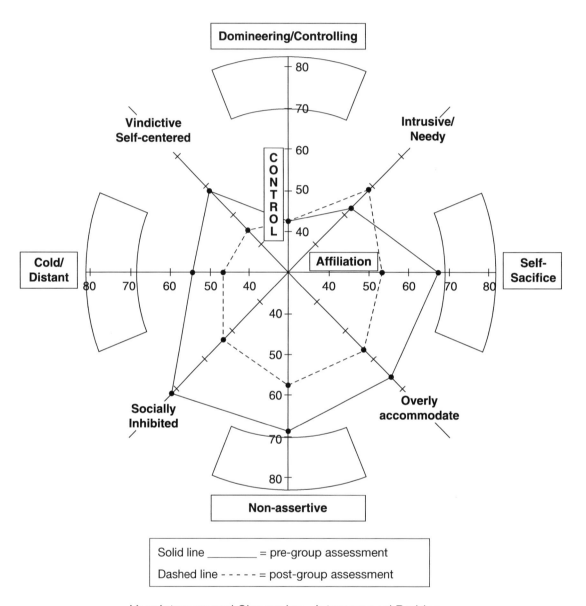

Your Interpersonal Circumplex—Interpersonal Problems

Horowitz et al. (2000)

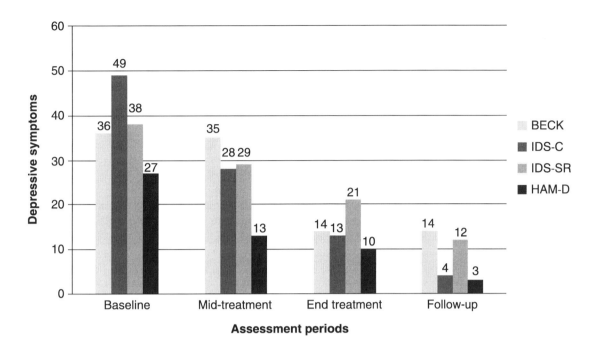

Changes in Depression Symptoms

On the Y axis: Beck is the Beck Depression Inventory (Beck et al., 1961); IDS-C is the Inventory of Depression Symptoms, clinician interview form; IDS-SR is the Inventory of Depression Symptoms, self-report form (Trivedi et al., 2004); HAM-D is the 17-item Hamilton Depression Rating Scale (Hamilton, 1960). On the X axis: Baseline measures were taken prior to beginning group. Mid-treatment assessment was ten weeks after the start of group. End of treatment assessment was after 20 weeks of group. Follow-up assessment was 12 weeks after the end of group therapy. All measures of depressive symptoms improved with maintenance at the three-month follow-up and remission of symptoms according to a semi-structured clinical interview.

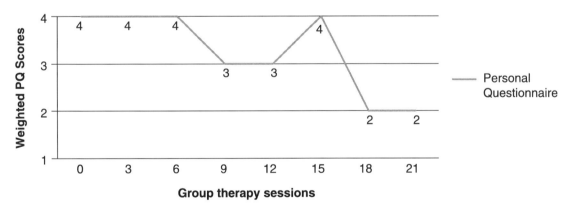

Personal Questionnaire Summary

Alice's ratings for the TH changed over time as she adhered, by week 20 of Group-CBASP, to the following sentence: *"More often than not, I feel that if I express negative feelings like anger, then others will not judge me negatively, I am good enough."*

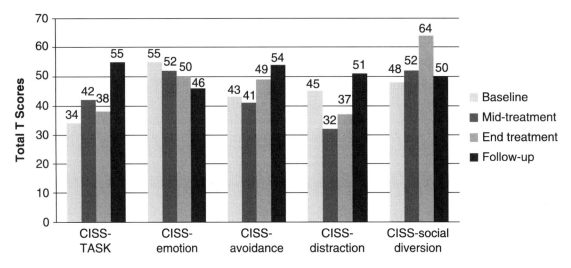

Changes in Coping Strategies

On the Y axis: The total T score obtained on The Coping Inventory for Stressful Situations (CISS) (Endler & Parker, 1999), using norms for a non-psychiatric population. On the X axis: the sub-scales measured at each of the four following assessment periods: baseline measures were taken prior to beginning group; mid-treatment assessment was ten weeks after the start of group; end of treatment assessment was after 20 weeks of group; follow-up assessment was 12 weeks after the end of group therapy.

The results indicate a greater use of task-oriented coping strategies that have been developed during Group-CBASP and greatly increased by the three-month follow-up. Also, a decrease in emotion-oriented coping over the four assessment periods reaches a level below the average for a non-psychiatric population. Avoidance strategies increase slightly over the course of treatment, with preference given to social diversion as a coping strategy to avoid stress, which is adaptive for depressive patients to help break the isolation. Alice learned that she does not need to become very angry when she needs to express herself or disagree. She learned to accept a DO that is within her control and to accept that she cannot have control over another person.

Alice was very satisfied with her experience in group therapy. She learned how to focus on what she wants in an interpersonal interaction and sees that this is essential for her recovery. She is also more assertive and does not attribute as much importance to pleasing others in order to feel esteemed. She is more focused on gaining control over her own life and understands that she has been very demanding of herself. Alice also learned to place importance on obtaining pleasure and rewards from her activities and to give herself credit for her achievements. She now is more satisfied with her accomplishments and is learning to pace herself on a daily basis.

HANDOUT 17

THE SITUATIONAL ANALYSIS (SA) (FOR INDIVIDUAL THERAPY)

(Coping Survey Questionnaire—CSQ)

Name: _____

Therapist: _____

Date of Situational Event: _____

Date of Therapy Session: _____

Instructions: Select one stressful interpersonal event that you have confronted during the past week and describe it using the format below. Please try to fill out <u>all</u> parts of the form. Your therapist will assist you in reviewing this Situational Analysis during your next therapy session.

Situational Area: Family_____ **Work/School**_____ **Social**_____

Step 1. Describe <u>WHAT</u> happened: (Write who said or did what, then describe clearly how the interpersonal event ended—the final point.)

© J.P. McCullough, Jr. (2000). *Treatment for Chronic Depression: Cognitive Behavioral Analysis System of Psychotherapy (CBASP)*. New York: Guilford Press. Copyright of Guilford Press. Reprinted with permission of The Guilford Press

HANDOUT 17

Step 2. How did you <u>INTERPRET</u> what happened during the event?: (How do you "read" what happened; what thoughts did you have which indicate how the interpersonal event unravelled; what did this event mean to you—what sense did you make of what happened, from the beginning to the end? Make a sentence for each interpretation. Try to limit yourself to three interpretations.)

a. _____

b. _____

c. _____

Step 3. Describe what you <u>DID</u> during the situation, your behaviors: (How did you say what you said? What were some of your nonverbal behaviors, tone of voice, eye contact, etc?)

Step 4. Describe <u>HOW</u> the event came out for <u>You</u> (The <u>ACTUAL OUTCOME</u> (AO)): (What *ACTUALLY* happened at the end of this exchange; what was observable?)

Step 5. Describe how you <u>Wanted</u> the event to come out for you (The <u>DESIRED OUTCOME</u> (DO)): (How would you have *WANTED* the event to come out for you? What *goal* would you have wanted to achieve, that is realistic, attainable and depends on you? Describe it in behavioral terms.

Step 6. Did you get what you wanted? YES___ NO___ Why or why not?

Explain why you think you do not get what you want in similar situations:

_____
_____

<u>My Action Interpretation</u>: Write out a thought that you need to tell yourself that will help you reach your goal, your DO, in this particular interpersonal situation described in step 1.

_____
_____

© J.P. McCullough, Jr. (2000). *Treatment for Chronic Depression: Cognitive Behavioral Analysis System of Psychotherapy (CBASP)*. New York: Guilford Press. Copyright of Guilford Press. Reprinted with permission of The Guilford Press

HANDOUT 9

THE SITUATIONAL ANALYSIS (SA)
(FOR GROUP THERAPY)

(Coping Survey Questionnaire—CSQ)

Your Name: _____

Name of person reporting the situation: _____

Therapist: _____

Date of Situational Event: _____

Date of Therapy Session: _____

Instructions: Select one stressful interpersonal event that you have confronted during the past week and describe it using the format below. Please try to fill out <u>all</u> parts of the form. Your therapist will assist you in reviewing this Situational Analysis during your next therapy session.

Situational Area: Family_____   Work/School_____   Social_____

Step 1. Describe <u>WHAT</u> happened: (Write who said or did what, then describe clearly how the interpersonal event ended—the final point.)
Note to group members: The person reporting the situation speaks, the other group members write down what he or she said about the situation.

Adapted to group therapy from: J.P. McCullough, Jr. (2000). *Treatment for Chronic Depression: Cognitive Behavioral Analysis System of Psychotherapy (CBASP).* New York: Guilford Press, page 107. Adapted with permission of The Guilford Press

HANDOUT 9

Step 2. How did you <u>INTERPRET</u> what happened during the event? (How do you "read" what happened; what thoughts did you have which indicate how the interpersonal event unraveled from the beginning to the end of this exchange? Make a sentence for each interpretation. Try to limit yourself to three interpretations.)

Note to group members: If the situation in step 1 is not yours but that of another group member, then imagine yourself in a similar situation and write a thought that you might have experienced in such an exchange. Write at least one sentence.

a. _____

_____

b. _____

_____

c. _____

_____

Step 3. Describe what you <u>DID</u> during the situation, your behaviors: (How did you say what you said? What were some of your nonverbal behaviors, tone of voice, eye contact, etc?)

Note to group members: We are describing here the behaviors of the person reporting the situation in step 1 (name the person), we are not describing the behaviors of other group members in their imagined situations. How do you think she or he behaved?

Step 4. Describe <u>HOW</u> the event came out for <u>You</u> (The <u>ACTUAL OUTCOME</u> (AO)): (What *ACTUALLY* happened at the end of this exchange; what was observable? Write one complete sentence describing observable behaviors.)

Note to group members: Now we are looking at the AO for the person who reported the situation in step 1 (name the person).

Adapted to group therapy from: J.P. McCullough, Jr. (2000). *Treatment for Chronic Depression: Cognitive Behavioral Analysis System of Psychotherapy (CBASP)*. New York: Guilford Press, page 107. Adapted with permission of The Guilford Press

HANDOUT 9

Step 5. Describe how you <u>Wanted</u> the event to come out for you (The <u>DESIRED OUTCOME</u> (DO)): (How would you have <u>*WANTED*</u> the event to come out for you? What *goal* would you have wanted to achieve, that is realistic, attainable and depends on you? Describe it in behavioral terms using a complete sentence.

Note to group members: Here, again, if the situation in step 1 is not yours, then imagine yourself in the same situation as you did in step 2 and now think of your DO for yourself. How would you have wanted the situation to end?

Step 6. Did you get what you wanted? YES___ NO___ Why or why not? Explain why you think you do not get what you want in similar situations:

Note to group members: Every group member can also think about whether he or she would get what he or she wants in a similar situation.

_____
_____
_____
_____
_____
_____

After the Remediation Phase of the exercise, identify:
<u>My Action Interpretation</u>: **Write out a thought that you need to tell yourself (like a coach speaking to you in your head) that will help you reach your goal, your DO, in this particular interpersonal situation described in step 1.**

Note to group members: Even if the situation is not yours in step 1, think about what your internal coach needs to tell you to reach your own DO.

_____
_____
_____
_____
_____
_____
_____

Adapted to group therapy from: J.P. McCullough, Jr. (2000). *Treatment for Chronic Depression: Cognitive Behavioral Analysis System of Psychotherapy (CBASP)*. New York: Guilford Press, page 107. Adapted with permission of The Guilford Press

114 APPENDICES

EXAMPLE OF A SITUATIONAL ANALYSIS (SA)

Patient: <u>Mary</u>

Therapist: <u>Dr. Smith</u>

Date of Situational Event: <u>January 30, 2005</u>

Date of Therapy Session: <u>February 2, 2005</u>

<u>Instructions</u>: Select one stress event that you have confronted during the past week and describe it using the format below. Please try to fill out <u>all</u> parts of the questionnaire. Your therapist will assist you in reviewing this Situational Analysis during your next therapy session.

Situational Area: Family_____   Work/School_____   Social <u>X</u>

1. Describe <u>what</u> happened:

   Attended the company picnic. The company photographer was taking pictures of everyone. He took Susan, Jane, Phyllis' pictures but not mine. [ENDPOINT] Camera man never offered to take my picture, and I never got my picture taken at the picnic.

2. How did you <u>interpret</u> what happened:

   a. The photographer doesn't like me (*mind read*: inaccurate, irrelevant)

   b. I never get what I want (to get my picture taken) (*irrelevant*: not situationally anchored)

   ** (*Add Action Interpretation*) Got to ask for what I want!**

3. Describe what you <u>did</u> during the situation:

   Said nothing to change the situation. Tried to be friendly with my colleagues.

** (*Add assertive behavior*) Ask to have my picture taken.**

4. Describe <u>how</u> the event came out for you (*AO*):

   I never got my picture taken at the picnic.

5. Describe how you <u>wanted</u> the event to come out for you (*DO*):

   Wanted to have my picture taken at the company picnic.

6. RATE: Did you get what you wanted? YES_____   NO <u>X</u>

© J.P. McCullough, Jr. (2000). *Treatment for Chronic Depression: Cognitive Behavioral Analysis System of Psychotherapy (CBASP)*. New York: Guilford Press. Copyright of Guilford Press. Reprinted with permission of The Guilford Press

HANDOUT 18

THE SITUATIONAL ANALYSIS (SA)
(ONE-PAGE POCKET-BOOK FORM)

Coping Survey Questionnaire—CSQ

Patient: _____

Therapist: _____

Date of Situational Event: _____

Date of Therapy Session: _____

<u>Instructions</u>: Select one stressful interpersonal event that you have confronted during the past week and describe it using the format below.

Step 1. Describe <u>what</u> happened: (Write who said or did what, then describe clearly how the event ended—the final point)

_____
_____
_____

Step 2. How did you <u>interpret</u> what happened: (How do you "read" what happened; what did this event mean to you?)

a. _____
b. _____
c. _____

Step 3. Describe what you <u>did</u> during the situation: (How did you say what you said? What were some of your behaviors, tone of voice, eye contact, etc.?)

_____

Step 4. Describe <u>how</u> the event came out for you (Actual Outcome): (What *actually* happened? Describe in such a way that an observer would have seen.

_____

Step 5. Describe how you <u>wanted</u> the event to come out for you (Desired Outcome): (How would you have <u>wanted</u> the event to come out for you? What <u>goal</u> would you have wanted to achieve, that is realistic and attainable? Describe it in behavioral terms.

_____

Step 6. RATE: Did you get what you wanted? YES____ NO____ Why or why not?

<u>My Action Interpretation:</u>

_____
_____

© J.P. McCullough, Jr. (2000). *Treatment for Chronic Depression: Cognitive Behavioral Analysis System of Psychotherapy (CBASP)*. New York: Guilford Press. Copyright of Guilford Press. Reprinted with permission of The Guilford Press

HANDOUT 11

FUTURE SITUATIONAL ANALYSIS (SA)

A future SA is used when you are thinking about what you want to say to or do with someone in the near future. In a future SA you will focus first on what you want, on your goal in the exchange you plan to have, within a specific *"slice of time"* with another person.

Step 1: Formulate a "behavioral" Desired Outcome (DO) (something that you can do: a *realistic* DO):

_____

_____

_____

Step 2: Write the "interpretations/reads" that must be in place to achieve the DO (you will need one **Action Read** that can be repeated to yourself):

_____

_____

_____

Step 3: Identify the "behaviors" that must be present to achieve the DO (you may need to do some *role-playing*):

_____

_____

_____

_____

Other suggestions:

(1) Don't worry about an Actual Outcome (AO) (it is a future event)
(2) Keep the SA simple—not complicated
(3) Review the Future SA after the situation has taken place

Adapted from J. P. McCullough, Jr. (2000). *Treatment for Chronic Depression: CBASP*. New York: Guilford Press. Copyright Guilford Press. Reprinted with permission of The Guilford Press

HANDOUT 10

SITUATIONAL ANALYSIS (SA): REMEDIATION PHASE

Now, let's go back into the situation that you described in step 1 of your SA and see what you might have changed to get what you wanted.

Step 1:

A- We first look at your interpretations. In the first interpretation, you said . . .

- Is this interpretation <u>grounded</u> in the event? Does the interpretation reflect what actually happened in this situation? If so, it is a relevant interpretation. A relevant interpretation plants your feet solidly in the event and helps achieve your DO.
- Is this interpretation true or <u>accurate</u>? I mean, do you think the interpretation accurately describes what is happening between you and the other person, or something that is happening in you: your feelings, thoughts, etc.?

<u>Rule</u>: If your interpretation is relevant and accurate, we will keep it. If it is relevant but not accurate, we will modify it. If it is neither relevant nor accurate, we will not address it further, and instead accept that it is not helpful in achieving your DO.

- Finally, how does this interpretation help you get to your Desired Outcome, that is, to what you want in that situation? If it doesn't help you get there, can we eliminate it?

<u>Rule</u>: If you now find that your Desired Outcome is unattainable or unrealistic after revising an interpretation, you need to revise the Desired Outcome first before continuing.

Now do the same with the second and third interpretations . . .

B- Now you may need an *<u>ACTION INTERPRETATION</u>*, which will prepare you to move toward getting what you want. This is a thought that you say to yourself about what you need to do to reach your Desired Outcome, your goal.

Step 2:

Now that you have revised your interpretations and perhaps found an *Action Interpretation*, how would your behavior have changed if you had used these revised or new interpretations?

If you had behaved this way, would you have gotten what you wanted, that is, your DO?

© J.P. McCullough, Jr. (2000). *Treatment for Chronic Depression: Cognitive Behavioral Analysis System of Psychotherapy (CBASP)*. New York: Guilford Press, pp. 282–284. Copyright of Guilford Press. Reprinted with permission of The Guilford Press

FORM 7

FORM FOR SCORING THE SELF-ADMINISTERED INTERPERSONAL DISCRIMINATION EXERCISE (SAD-IDE)

IDE Goals: (a) The first goal is to increase the safety stimulus value of group members and heal *earlier trauma* as well as a history of *psychological insults*; (b) the second goal is to open interpersonal relationships between group members to new growth possibilities by making explicit the differences between older toxic relationships and the present relationships within the group. The IDE is a four-step procedure that patients are taught to self-administer.

Sad-IDE Rating Scale Scoring Criterion: A step "hit" is scored when a step is completed without any assistance from the therapist. The "IDE criterion score" is 4/4 hits.

Patient: _____   Number/Date of Session ____/____

Scoring for Each of the Four Steps	Yes (✓)	No (✗)
Step 1. Patient accurately describes the Significant Other(s)' behavior in the *hot spot* and the consequences that ensued.	___	___
Step 2. Patient accurately describes the behavior of group members (how group members reacted to the patient) in the in-session situational context.	___	___
Step 3. Patient accurately compares and contrasts the behavior of group members with that of the Significant Other(s).	___	___
Step 4. Patient accurately describes the emotional and behavioral options now available to him/her within the group that were not available earlier with the Significant Other(s).	___	___
Total the number of "Yes" ratings for Rating Score:	___	

© McCullough et al., (2010). A method for conducting intensive psychological studies with early-onset chronically depressed patients. *American Journal of Psychotherapy, 64*(4), 317–337

APPENDICES **119**

FORM 8

PATIENT PERFORMANCE RATING FORM (PPRF)
FOR SITUATIONAL ANALYSIS (SA)

GENERAL INSTRUCTIONS

The goal is to rate what the patient has been able to do with SA by himself/herself during the group therapy session *without* assistance from the therapist. A perfect score of five "hits" denotes that the patient has completed *both* the Elicitation and Remediation Phases of the SA without any significant prompting or correction. The SA is a five-step procedure that patients are taught to self-administer.

Patient: _____   Number/Date of Session _____/_____

Scoring for Each of the Five Steps   Yes (✓)   No (✗)

Step 1. The situational event was relevant to
a significantly stressful situation and had a
beginning and an endpoint that was stated
in behavioral terms.   ___   ___

Step 2. The patient produced relevant and accurate
interpretations of the events occurring *during*
the situation and without prompts or corrective
remarks from the therapist. The interpretation(s)
accurately reflected what was going on in the
situation.   ___   ___

Step 3. The patient's behaviors during the situation
were appropriately related to the DO, or the patient
identified such behaviors without prompts from
the therapist.   ___   ___

Step 4. The patient stated in clear behavioral terms an
AO for the situation (reiteration of the endpoint of the
situation in step 1).   ___   ___

Step 5. The patient stated a realistic and attainable
DO that was expressed in behavioral terms.   ___   ___

Total the number of "Yes/hit" ratings for Rating Score: ___/Yes Hits

© J.P. McCullough, Jr. (2000). *Treatment for Chronic Depression: Cognitive Behavioral Analysis System of Psychotherapy (CBASP)*. New York: Guilford Press. Copyright of Guilford Press. Reprinted with permission of The Guilford Press

The PPRF is another means to assess the degree to which patients are learning the social problem-solving algorithm that is SA. The goal is for patients to eventually learn to perform SA independently with no therapist or other group member assistance, but this may take several sessions to achieve. There is typically a "learning curve" with a gradual slope upwards. Some therapist "process" input (social discourse) is needed to facilitate the flow of the SA performance. Such things as "good," "you've got that right," or other reflective comments can be helpful to facilitate the SA, however if there is extensive *active intervention* or *teaching the method*, this does not count as a "hit" for the patient. Direct "corrective" comments or "teaching the method" would constitute *intervention*. Comments that encouraged or positively reinforced the patient's performance during the SA would fall under the rubric of *reflection*.

Accurate and relevant interpretations don't necessarily have to take the patient to the goal box (DO), and should *not* be revised. However, *at least one* interpretation must actively take the patient to the goal box (DO) for step 2 to be scored as a "hit." We usually think of this type of read as an *Action Interpretation*. Without at least one interpretation contributing directly to the attainment of the DO, step 2 (Interpretation Step) cannot be scored as a "hit." The patient may self-remediate his/her SA during the Remediation Phase and add an Action Interpretation and be given a "hit" for step 2 (but *without intervention* on the part of the therapist).

The patient will NOT be given credit for step 5 (DO) unless step 2 contains one interpretation that will take the person to the goal box (DO); and the patient cannot be given credit for step 3 unless it contains behaviors that also contribute directly to the attainment of the DO. *Thus, steps 2, 3, and 5 are linked—can't have a "hit" in any one of these three steps unless the patient has successfully "hit" all three either during the Elicitation or Remediation Phases.*

Step 1 must have a clear beginning point and clear ending point and a story in between (without embellishments such as "motives," "jumping out of the slice of time," "explanations of why I was in the situation in the first place," etc.). In step 4, the AO cannot be scored as "hit" unless it is stated in one behavioral sentence AND unless it reflects the *endpoint* of step 1.

The major goal of learning SA is to teach the CBASP patient to "keep his/her eye on the target" in interpersonal situations, and to help him/her adjust and reset another situational goal when it becomes obvious that he/she will not obtain their first-choice DO.

FORM 9

CIRCUMPLEX MEASURES

Author: K. D. Locke, Ph.D. – Professor, Department of Psychology and Communication Studies, University of Idaho. Moscow ID 83844-3043.

Download circumplex scales free at www.webpages.uidaho.edu/klocke/

Hand-scoring formulas for the Circumplex Scale of Interpersonal Efficacy (CSIE) and the Circumplex Scale of Interpersonal Values (CSIV-32 item form):

* **Compute CSIE raw octant scores (the average of four items). The numbers within parentheses refer to the number of the item on the CSIE.**

Compute csiePA = (csie04+csie12+csie20+csie28)/4.
Compute csieBC = (csie07+csie15+csie23+csie31)/4.
Compute csieDE = (csie02+csie10+csie18+csie26)/4.
Compute csieFG = (csie05+csie13+csie21+csie29)/4.
Compute csieHI = (csie08+csie16+csie24+csie32)/4.
Compute csieJK = (csie03+csie11+csie19+csie27)/4.
Compute csieLM = (csie06+csie14+csie22+csie30)/4.
Compute csieNO = (csie01+csie09+csie17+csie25)/4.
COMPUTE csieAGENCY = 0.414*(csiePA-csieHI+(.707*(csieBC+csieNO-csieFG-csieJK))).
COMPUTE csieAFFILIATION = 0.414*(csieLM-csieDE+(.707*(csieNO+csieJK-csieFG-csieBC))).

* **Compute CSIV short form raw octant scores (the average of four items). The numbers within parentheses refer to the number of the item on the 32-item CSIV.**

Compute csivPA = (csiv01+csiv09+csiv17+csiv25)/4.
Compute csivBC = (csiv04+csiv12+csiv20+csiv28)/4.
Compute csivDE = (csiv07+csiv15+csiv23+csiv31)/4.
Compute csivFG = (csiv02+csiv10+csiv18+csiv26)/4.
Compute csivHI = (csiv05+csiv13+csiv21+csiv29)/4.
Compute csivJK = (csiv08+csiv16+csiv24+csiv32)/4.
Compute csivLM = (csiv03+csiv11+csiv19+csiv27)/4.
Compute csivNO = (csiv06+csiv14+csiv22+csiv30)/4.
COMPUTE csivAGENCY = 0.414*(csivPA-csivHI+(.707*(csivBC+csivNO-csivFG-csivJK))).
COMPUTE csivAFFILIATION = 0.414*(csivLM-csivDE+(.707*(csivNO+csivJK-csivFG-csivBC))).

FORM 10

NORMS FOR THE CIRCUMPLEX SCALE OF INTERPERSONAL VALUES (CSIV)

The following norms are based on the responses of 1,200 University of Idaho undergraduates.

	Mean	Std. Deviation
PA (+A)	2.53	(.63)
BC (+A-C)	1.38	(.71)
DE (-C)	1.10	(.70)
FG (-A-C)	1.66	(.78)
HI (-A)	1.77	(.75)
JK (-A+C)	2.67	(.71)
LM (+C)	2.83	(.69)
NO (+A+C)	2.93	(.57)

NORMS FOR THE CIRCUMPLEX SCALE OF INTERPERSONAL EFFICACY (CSIE)

The following are CSIE means and standard deviations from the general population samples obtained through Amazon's Mechanical Turk described in Studies 3–4 of the following article (Locke & Adamic, 2012).

	Mean	Std. Deviation
PA (+A)	2.53	(.88)
BC (+A-C)	2.16	(.83)
DE (-C)	2.15	(.87)
FG (-A-C)	2.62	(.70)
HI (-A)	2.49	(.72)
JK (-A+C)	3.11	(.63)
LM (+C)	2.77	(.68)
NO (+A+C)	2.44	(.80)

n = 772 females, 449 males.

Locke & Adamic (2012)

HANDOUT 13

YOUR INTERPERSONAL CIRCUMPLEX—VALUES/MOTIVES

It is important to me that . . .

I am obeyed

I attack back
when attacked

I express
myself openly

AGENCY

Others
keep their
distance

AFFILIATION

I feel
connected
to others

I do not say
something stupid

Others approve
of me

I do what others
want me to do

Locke (2000)

HANDOUT 14

YOUR INTERPERSONAL CIRCUMPLEX–EFFICACY

Locke & Sadler (2007)

REFERENCES

Akiskal, H. S., Rosenthal, T. L., Haykal, R. F., Lemmi, H., Rosenthal, R. H., & Scott-Strauss, A. (1980). Characterological depressions. Clinical and sleep EEG findings separating "sub-affective dysthymias" from "character spectrum disorders." *Archives of General Psychiatry*, *37*(7), 777–783.

Akiskal, H. S., King, D., Rosenthal, T. L., Robinson, D., & Scott-Strauss, A. (1981). Chronic depressions. Part 1. Clinical and familial characteristics in 137 probands. *Journal of Affective Disorders*, *3*(3), 297–315. doi: 0165-0327(81)90031-8 [pii]

APA (2013). *Diagnostic and Statistical Manual of Mental Disorders – DSM-5* (Fifth Edition). Washington, DC: American Psychiatric Publishing.

Arnow, B. A., & Constantino, M. J. (2003). Effectiveness of psychotherapy and combination treatment for chronic depression. *Journal of Clinical Psychology*, *59*(8), 893–905.

Ball, S. G., Otto, M. W., Pollack, M. H., & Rosenbaum, J. F. (1994). Predicting prospective episodes of depression in patients with panic disorder: A longitudinal study. *Journal of Consulting and Clinical Psychology*, *62*(2), 359–365. doi: 10.1037/0022-006X.62.2.359

Bandura, A. (1997). *Self-Efficacy: The Exercise of Control*. New York: Freeman.

Bandura, A. (2012). On the functional properties of perceived self-efficacy revisited. *Journal of Management*, *38*(1), 9–44.

Beck, A. T., Ward, C. H. Mendelson, M., Mock, J., & Erbaugh, J. (1961). An inventory for measuring depression. *Archives of General Psychiatry*, *4*, 561–571.

Berlim, M. T., & Turecki, G. (2007). Definition, assessment, and staging of treatment-resistant refractory major depression: A review of current concepts and methods. *Canadian Journal of Psychiatry*, *52*(1), 46–54.

Bockting, C. L. H., Schene, A. H., Spinhoven, P., Koeter, M. W. J., Wouters, L. F., Huyser, J., & Kamphuis, J. H. (2005). Preventing relapse/recurrence in recurrent depression with cognitive therapy: A randomized controlled trial. *Journal of Consulting and Clinical Psychology*, *73*(4), 647–657. doi: 10.1037/0022-006X.73.4.647

Bornstein, R. F. (1992). The dependent personality: Developmental, social, and clinical pespectives. *Psychological Bulletin*, *112*(1), 3–23.

Brakemeier, E. L., Engel, V., Schramm, E., Zobel, I., Schmidt, T., Hautzinger, M., . . . Normann, C. (2011). Feasibility and outcome of cognitive behavioral analysis system of psychotherapy (CBASP) for chronically depressed inpatients: A pilot study. *Psychotherapy and Psychosomatics, 80*(3), 191–194. doi: 10.1159/000320779

Bristow, M., & Bright, J. (1995). Group cognitive therapy in chronic depression: Results from two intervention studies. *Behavioural and Cognitive Psychotherapy, 23*, 373–380.

Cain, N. M., Ansell, E. B., Wright, A. G. C., Hopwood, C. J., Thomas, K. M., Pinto, A., . . . Grilo, C. M. (2012). Interpersonal pathoplasticity in the course of major depression. *Journal of Consulting and Clinical Psychology, 80*, 78–86.

Constantino, M. J., Manber, R., DeGeorge, J., McBride, C., Ravitz, P., Zuroff, D., & . . . Arnow, B. A. (2008). Interpersonal styles of chronically depressed outpatients: Profiles and therapeutic change. *Psychotherapy: Theory, Research, Practice, Training, 45*, 491–506. doi: 10.1037/a0014335

Constantino, M. J., Laws, H., Arnow, B. A., Klein, D. N., Rothbaum, B. O., & Manber, R. (2012). The relation between changes in patients' interpersonal impact messages and outcome in treament for chronic depression. *Journal of Consulting and Clinical Psychology, 80*(3), 354–364.

Coyne, J. C. (1976). Toward an interactional description of depression. *Psychiatry Research, 39*(1), 28–40.

Cuijpers, P., Van Straten, A., Andersson, G., & Van Oppen, P. (2008). Psychotherapy for depression in adults: A meta-analysis of comparative outcome studies. *Journal of Consulting and Clinical Psychology, 76*(6), 909–922. doi: 10.1037/a0013075

Cuijpers, P., Van Straten, A., & Warmerdam, L. (2008). Are individual and group treatments equally effective in the treatment of depression in adults? A meta-analysis. *European Journal of Psychiatry, 22*(1), 38–51.

Cuijpers, P., Van Straten, A., Schuurmans, J., Van Oppen, P., Hollon, S. D., & Andersson, G. (2010). Psychotherapy for chronic major depression and dysthymia: A meta-analysis. *Clinical Psychology Review, 30*(1), 51–62. doi: http://dx.doi.org/10.1016/j.cpr.2009.09.003

Dimidjian, S., Hollon, S. D., Dobson, K. S., Schmaling, K. B., Kohlenberg, R. J., Addis, M. E., . . . Jacobson, N. S. (2006). Randomized trial of behavioral activation, cognitive therapy, and antidepressant medication in the acute treatment of adults with major depression. *Journal of Consulting and Clinical Psychology, 74*(4), 658–670. doi: 2006-09621-003 [pii] 10.1037/0022-006X.74.4.658

Dube, S. R., Anda, R. F., Felitti, V. J., Chapman, D. P., Williamson, D. F., & Giles, W. H. (2001). Childhood abuse, household dysfunction, and the risk of attempted suicide throughout the life span: Findings from the Adverse Childhood Experiences Study. *JAMA, 286*(24), 3089–3096.

Endler, N. S., & Parker, J. D. A. (1999). *Coping Inventory for Stressful Situations (CISS)*. Toronto: Multi-Health Systems Inc.

Enns, M. W., & Cox, B. J. (2005). Psychosocial and clinical predictors of symptom persistence vs remission in Major Depressive Disorder. *Canadian Journal of Psychiatry, 50*(12), 769–777.

Fava, G. A., Ruini, C., & Belaise, C. (2007). The concept of recovery in major depression. *Psychological Medicine, 37*(3), 307–317. doi: S0033291706008981 [pii] 10.1017/S0033291706008981

Grosse Holtforth, M., Altenstein, D., Ansell, E., Schneider, C., & Caspar, F. (2012). Impact messages of depressed outpatients as perceived by their significant others: Profiles, therapeutic change, and relationship to outcome. *Journal of Clinical Psychology, 68*(3), 319–333.

Hames, J. L., Hagan, C. R., & Joiner, T. E. (2013). Interpersonal processes in depression. *Annual Review of Clinical Psychology, 9*, 355–377.

Hamilton, M. (1960). A rating scale for depression. *Journal of Neurology, Neurosurgery and Psychiatry, 23*, 56–62.

Harley, R., Sprich, S., Safren, S., Jacobo, M., & Fava, M. (2008). Adaptation of dialectical behavior therapy skills training group for treatment-resistant depression. *Journal of Nervous and Mental Disease, 196*(2), 136–143. doi: 10.1097/NMD.0b013e318162a a3f00005053-200802000-00008 [pii]

Heim, C., & Nemeroff, C. B. (2001). The role of childhood trauma in the neurobiology of mood and anxiety disorders: Preclinical and clinical studies. *Biological Psychiatry, 49*(12), 1023–1039.

Hölzel, L., Härter, M., Reese, C., & Kriston, L. (2011). Risk factors for chronic depression – A systematic review. *Journal of Affective Disorders, 129*(1–3), 1–13. doi: http://dx.doi.org/10.1016/j.jad.2010.03.025

Horowitz, L. M. (2004). *Interpersonal Foundations of Psychopathology*. Washington DC: American Psychological Association.

Horowitz, L. M., Alden, L. E., Wiggins, J. S., & Pincus, A. L. (2000). *Inventory of Interpersonal Problems (IIP) – Manual*. San Antonion, TX: The Psychological Corporation, a Harcourt Assessment Company.

Horowitz, L. M., Wilson, K. R., Turan, B., Zolotsev, P., Constantino, M. J., & Henderson, L. (2006). How interpersonal motives clarify the meaning of interpersonal behavior: A Revised Circumplex Model. *Personality and Social Psychology Review, 10*(1), 67–86.

Inoue, Y., Tonooka, Y., Yamada, K., & Kanba, S. (2004). Deficiency of theory of mind in patients with remitted mood disorder. *Journal of Affective Disorders, 82*(3), 403–409. doi: 10.1016/j.jad.2004.04.004

Inoue, Y., Yamada, K., & Kanba, S. (2006). Deficit in theory of mind is a risk for relapse of major depression. *Journal of Affective Disorders, 95*(1–3), 125–127. doi: 10.1016/j.jad.2006.04.018

Joiner, T. E., Alfano, M. S., & Metalsky, G. I. (1992). When depression breeds contempt: Reassurance seeking, self-esteem, and rejection of depressed college students by their roommates. *Journal of Abnormal Psychology, 101*, 165–173.

Keller, M. B., & Boland, R. J. (1998). Implications of failing to achieve successful long-term maintenance treatment of recurrent unipolar major depression. *Biological Psychiatry, 44*(5), 348–360. doi: S0006-3223(98)00110-3 [pii]

Keller, M. B., Klerman, G. L., Lavori, P. W., Coryell, W., Endicott, J., & Taylor, J. (1984). Long-term outcome of episodes of major depression. Clinical and public health significance. *JAMA, 252*(6), 788–792.

Keller, M. B., McCullough, J. P., Jr., Klein, D. N., Arnow, B., Dunner, D. L., Gelenberg, A. J., . . . Zajecka, J. (2000). A comparison of nefazodone, the cognitive behavioral-analysis system of psychotherapy, and their combination for the treatment of chronic depression. *The New England Journal of Medicine, 342*(20), 1462–1470. doi: 10.1056/NEJM200005183422001

Kendler, K. S., Kessler, R. C., Walters, E. E., MacLean, C., Neale, M. C., Heath, A. C., & Eaves, L. J. (1995). Stressful life events, genetic liability, and onset of an episode of major depression in women. *American Journal of Psychiatry, 152*(6), 833–842.

Kessler, R. C., Berglund, P., Delmer, O., Jin, R., Koretz, D., Merikangas, K. R., . . . Wang, P. S. (2003). The epidemiology of major depressive disorder: Results from the National Comorbidity Survey Replication (NCS-R). *JAMA, 289*(23), 3095–3105.

Kiesler, D. J., & Schmidt, J. A. (1993). *The Impact Message Inventory: Form IIA Octant Scale Version*. Palo Alto, CA: Mind Garden.

Klein, D. N., Schatzberg, A. F., McCullough, J. P., Keller, M. B., Dowling, F., Goodman, D., . . . Harrison, W. M. (1999). Early- versus late-onset dythymic disorder: comparison in outpatients with superimposed major depressive episodes. *Journal of Affective Disordorders, 52*(1–3), 187–196.

Klein, D. N., Santiago, N. J., Vivian, D., Blalock, J. A., Kocsis, J. H., Markowitz, J. C., . . . Keller, M. B. (2004). Cognitive-behavioral analysis system of psychotherapy as a maintenance treatment for chronic depression. *Journal of Consulting and Clinical Psychology, 72*(4), 681–688. doi: 10.1037/0022-006X.72.4.6812004-16970-014 [pii]

Kocsis, J. H., Gelenberg, A. J., Rothbaum, B. O., Klein, D. N., Trivedi, M. H., Manber, R., . . . Thase, M. E. (2009). Cognitive behavioral analysis system of psychotherapy and brief supportive psychotherapy for augmentation of antidepressant nonresponse in chronic depression: The REVAMP Trial. *Archives of General Psychiatry, 66*(11), 1178–1188. doi: 66/11/1178 [pii] 10.1001/archgenpsychiatry.2009.144

Komossa, K., Depping, A. M., Gaudchau, A., Kissling, W., & Leucht, S. (2010). Second-generation antipsychotics for major depressive disorder and dysthymia. *Cochrane Database of Systematic Reviews, (12):CD008121.*

Kornstein, S. G., & Schneider, R. K. (2001). Clinical features of treatment-resistant depression. *Journal of Clinical Psychiatry, 62*(16), 18–25.

Kriston, L., von Wolff, A., Westphal, A., Hölzel, L. P., & Härter, M. (2014). Efficacy and acceptability of acute treatments for persistent depressive disorder: A network meta-analysis. *Depression and Anxiety, 31*(8), 621–630. doi: 10.1002/da.22236

Kuehner, C., & Huffziger, S. (2012). Response styles to depressed mood affect the long-term course of psychosocial functioning in depressed patients. *Journal of Affective Disorders, 136,* 627–633.

Lam, D., Schuck, N., Smith, N., Farmer, A., & Checkley, S. (2003). Response style, interpersonal difficulties and social functioning in major depressive disorder. *Journal of Affective Disorders, 75,* 279–283.

Locke, K. D. (2000). Circumplex scales of interpersonal values: Reliability, and applicability to interpersonal problems and personality disorders. *Journal of Personality Assessment, 75*(2), 249–267.

Locke, K. D. (2006). Interpersonal circumplex measures. In S. Strack (Ed.), *Differentiating Normal and Abnormal Personality* (2nd Ed. pp. 383–400). New York: Springer.

Locke, K. D. (2011). Circumplex measures of interpersonal constructs. In L. M. Horowitz & S. Strack (Eds.), *Handbook of Interpersonal Psychology* (pp. 313–324). Hoboken, NJ.: John Wiley & Sons, Inc.

Locke, K. D., & Sadler, P. (2007). Self-efficacy, values, and complementarity in dyadic interactions: Integrating interpersonal and social-cognitive theory. *Personality and Social Psychology Bulletin, 33*(1), 94–109.

Locke, K. D., & Adamic, E. (2012). Interpersonal circumplex vector length and interpersonal decision making. *Personality and Individual Differences, 53,* 764–769.

Locke, K. D., Sayegh, L., Penberthy, J. K., Weber, C., Haentjens, K., & Turecki, G. (2015). Interpersonal circumplex profiles of persistent depression: Goals, self-efficacy, problems, and effects of group therapy. Submitted to the *Journal of Clinical Psychology.*

McCullough, J. P., Jr. (2000). *Treatment for Chronic Depression: Cognitive Behavioral Analysis System of Psychotherapy (CBASP).* New York: Guilford Press.

McCullough, J. P., Jr. (2001). *Skills Training Manual for Diagnosing and Treating Chronic Depression: Cognitive Behavioral Analysis System of Psychotherapy.* New York: Guilford Press.

McCullough, J. P., Jr. (2003). *Patient's Manual for CBASP.* New York: Guilford Press.

McCullough, J. P., Jr. (2006). *Treating Chronic Depression with Disciplined Personal Involvement: Cognitive Behavioral Analysis System of Psychotherapy (CBASP).* New York: Springer.

McCullough, J. P., Jr. (2008). *CBASP Intensive Training Workbook.* Department of Psychology. Virginia Commonwealth University. Richmond, Virginia 23284–2018.

McCullough, J. P., Jr., & Kasnetz, M. D. (1982). *Manual for the Construction and Scoring of the Personal Questionnaire.* Unpublished manuscript. Virginia Commonwealth University. Richmond, VA.

McCullough, J. P., Jr., & Penberthy, J. K. (2011). Cognitive behavioral analysis system of psychotherapy for chronic depression. In D. W. Springer, A. Rubin, & C. G. Beevers (Eds.),

Treatment of Depression in Adolescents and Adults (pp. 183–220). New Jersey: John Wiley & Sons, Inc.

McCullough, J. P., Jr., Lord, B. D., Conley, K. A., & Martin, A. M. (2010). A method for conducting intensive psychological studies with early-onset chronically depressed patients. *American Journal of Psychotherapy, 64*(4), 317–337.

McCullough, J. P., Jr., Lord, B. D., Martin, A. M., Conley, K. A., Schramm, E., & Klein, D. N. (2011). The significant other history: An interpersonal-emotional history procedure used with the early-onset chronically depressed patient. *American Journal of Psychotherapy, 65*(3), 225–248.

McCullough, J. P., Jr., Schramm, E., & Penberthy, J. K. (2014). *CBASP as a Distinctive Treatment for Persistent Depressive Disorder: Distinctive features (CBT Distinctive Features)*. London: Routledge.

Manber, R., Arnow, B., Blasey, C., Vivian, D., McCullough, J. P., Blalock, J. A., . . . Keller, M. B. (2003). Patient's therapeutic skill acquisition and response to psychotherapy, alone or in combination with medication. *Psychological Medicine, 33*(4), 693–702.

Matsunaga, M., Okamoto, Y., Suzuki, S., Kinoshita, A., Yoshimura, S., Yoshino, A., . . . Yamawaki, S. (2010). Psychosocial functioning in patients with Treatment-Resistant Depression after group cognitive behavioral therapy. *BMC Psychiatry, 10*, 22. doi: 1471-244X-10-22 [pii] 10.1186/1471-244X-10-22

Nemeroff, C. B., Heim, C. M., Thase, M. E., Klein, D. N., Rush, A. J., Schatzberg, A. F., . . . Keller, M. B. (2003). Differential responses to psychotherapy versus pharmacotherapy in patients with chronic forms of major depression and childhood trauma. *Proceedings of the National Academy of Sciences U S A, 100*(24), 14293–14296. doi: 10.1073/pnas.2336126100 2336126100 [pii]

Oei, T. P., & Dingle, G. (2008). The effectiveness of group cognitive behaviour therapy for unipolar depressive disorders. *Journal of Affective Disorders, 107*(1–3), 5–21. doi: S0165-0327(07)00271-6 [pii] 10.1016/j.jad.2007.07.018

Petty, S. C., Sachs-Ericsson, N., & Joiner Jr, T. E. (2004). Interpersonal functioning deficits: Temporary or stable characteristics of depressed individuals? *Journal of Affective Disorders, 81*(2), 115–122. doi: http://dx.doi.org/10.1016/S0165-0327(03)00158-7

Piaget, J. (1926). *The Language and Thought of the Child*. New York: Harcourt, Brace.

Piaget, J. (1981). *Intelligence and Affectivity: Their Relationship During Child Development*. Trans. & Ed. T. A. Brown & C. E. Kaegi. xiv, 77 pp. Oxford, England: Annual Reviews.

Pincus, A. L., & Gurtman, M. B. (1995). The three faces of interpersonal dependency: Structural analyses of self-report dependency measures. *Journal of Personality and Social Psychology, 69*(4), 744–758.

Pincus, A. L., & Wright, A. G. C. (2011). Interpersonal diagnosis of psychopathology. In L. M. Horowitz & S. Strack (Eds.), *Handbook of Interpersonal Psychology: Theory, Research, Assessment and Therapeutic Interventions* (pp. 359–381). New Jersey: John Wiley & Sons, Inc.

Quilty, L. C., Mainland, B. J., McBride, C. M., & Bagby, R. M. (2013). Interpersonal problems and impacts: Further evidence for the role of interpersonal functioning in treatment outcome in major depressive disorder. *Journal of Affective Disorders, 150*, 393–400.

Sackeim, H. A. (2001). The definition and meaning of treatment-resistant depression. *Journal of Clinical Psychiatry, 62 Suppl 16*, 10–17.

Saulsman, L. M., Coall, D. A., & Nathan, P. R. (2006). The association between depressive personality and treatment outcome for depression following a group cognitive-behavioral intervention. *Journal of Clinical Psychology, 62*(9), 1181–1196. doi: 10.1002/jclp.20278

Sayegh, L., Locke, K. D., Pistilli, D., Penberthy, J. K., Chachamovich, E., McCullough, J. P., Jr., & Turecki, G. (2012). Cognitive behavioural analysis system of psychotherapy for treatment-resistant depression: Adaptation to a group modality. *Behaviour Change, 29*(02), 97–108. doi: 10.1017/bec.2012.2

Schnell, K., Bluschke, S., Konradt, B., & Walter, H. (2011). Functional relations of empathy and mentalizing: An fMRI study on the neural basis if cognitive empathy. *NeuroImage, 54,* 1743–1754.

Schramm, E., Schneider, D., Zobel, I., van Calker, D., Dykierek, P., Kech, S., . . . Berger, M. (2008). Efficacy of interpersonal psychotherapy plus pharmacotherapy in chronically depressed inpatients. *Journal of Affective Disorders, 109*(1–2), 65–73. doi: S0165-0327(07)00357-6 [pii] 10.1016/j.jad.2007.10.013

Schramm, E., Zobel, I., Dykierek, P., Kech, S., Brakemeier, E. V., Külz, A., & Berger, M. (2011). Cognitive behavioral analysis system of psychotherapy versus interpersonal psychotherapy for early-onset chronic depression: A randomized pilot study. *Journal of Affective Disorders, 129,* 109–116.

Schramm, P. J., Zobel, I., Mönch, K., Schramm, E., & Michalak, J. (2014). WITHDRAWN: Sleep quality changes in chronically depressed patients treated with mindfulness-based cognitive therapy or cognitive behavioral analysis system for psychotherapy: a pilot study. *Sleep Medicine.*

Shapiro, M. B. (1961). A method of measuring psychological changes specific to the individual psychiatric patient. *British Journal of Medical Psychology, 34,* 151–155.

Shapiro, M. B., Litman, G. K., Nias, D. K. B., & Hendry, E. R. (1973). A clinician's approach to experimental research. *Journal of Clinical Psychology* (April), 165–169.

Shaver, P. R., & Mikulincer, M. (2011). An attachment-theory framework for conceptualizing interpersonal behavior. In L. M. Horowitz & S. Strack (Eds.), *Handbook of Interpersonal Psychology: Theory, Research, Assessment and Therapeutic Interventions* (pp. 17–35). New Jersey: John Wiley & Sons, Inc.

Sonawalla, S. B., & Fava, M. (2001). Severe depression: Is there a best approach? *CNS Drugs, 15*(10), 765–776. doi: 151003 [pii]

Swan, J., Sorrell, E., MacVicar, B., Durham, R., & Matthews, K. (2004). "Coping with depression": an open study of the efficacy of a group psychoeducational intervention in chronic, treatment-refractory depression. *Journal of Affective Disorders, 82*(1), 125–129. doi: S0165032703002258 [pii] 10.1016/j.jad.2003.09.002

Swan, J. S., Macvicar, R., Christmas, D., Durham, R., Rauchhaus, P., McCullough, J. P., Jr., & Matthews, K. (2014). Cognitive Behavioural Analysis System of Psychotherapy (CBASP) for chronic depression: clinical characteristics and six month clinical outcomes in an open case series. *Journal of Affective Disorders, 152–154,* 268–276. doi: 10.1016/j.jad.2013.09.024

Teismann, T., von Brachel, R., Hanning, S., Grillenberger, M., Hebermehl, L., Hornstein, I., & Willutzki, U. (2013). A randomized controlled trial on the effectiveness of a rumination-focused group treatment for residual depression. *Psychotherapy Research, 24*(1), 80–90. doi: 10.1080/10503307.2013.821636

Thase, M. E. (1997). Psychotherapy of refractory depressions. *Depress Anxiety, 5*(4), 190–201. doi: 10.1002/(SICI)1520-6394(1997)5:4<190::AID-DA5>3.0.CO;2-H [pii]

Thase, M. E., Friedman, E. S., & Howland, R. H. (2001). Management of treatment-resistant depression: Psychotherapeutic perspectives. *Journal of Clinical Psychiatry, 62 Suppl 18,* 18–24.

Trivedi, M. H., Rush, A. J., Ibrahim, H. M., Carmody, T. J., Biggs, M. M., Suppes, T., . . . Kashner, T. M. (2004). The Inventory of Depressive Symptomatology, Clinician Rating (IDS-C) and Self-Report (IDS-SR), and the Quick Inventory of Depressive Symptomatology, Clinician Rating (QIDS-C) and Self-Report (QIDS-SR) in public sector patients with mood disorders: a psychometric evaluation. *Psychological Medicine, 34*(1), 73–82.

von Wolff, A., Hölzel, L. P., Westphal, A., Härter, M., & Kriston, L. (2012). Combination of pharmacotherapy and psychotherapy in the treatment of chronic depression: a systematic review and meta-analysis. *BMC Psychiatry, 12,* 61. doi: http://dx.doi.org/10.1186%2F1471-244X-12-61

Weissman, M. M. (1999). *Social Adjustment Scale- Self-report (SAS-SR) – Technical Manual.* Toronto: Multi-Health Systems Inc.

Wiersma, J. E., Van Schaik, D. J. F., Hoogendorn, A. W., Dekker, J. J., Van, H. L., Schoevers, R. A., . . . Van Oppen, P. (2014). The effectiveness of the cognitive behavioral analysis system of psychotherapy for chronic depression: A randomized controlled trial. *Psychotherapy and Psychosomatics*, *83*(5), 263–269.

World Federation for Mental Health. (2012). Depression: A global crisis. World Mental Health Day, October 10: World Federation for Mental Health. Available at: http://wfmh. com/wp-content/uploads/2013/11/2012_wmhday_english.pdf

World Federation for Mental Health. (2015). Depression in the workplace. Report by Lundbeck. Available at http://wfmh.com/wp-content/uploads/2014/06/Depression-in-the-Workplace_PDF_v02.pdf

INDEX

Action Interpretation 8, 39, 46, 48, 71, 72, 114, 116, 121 *see also* interpretation
Activity Log 27, 31, 34, 35
Actual Outcome 8, 15, 48, 50, 116, 118
Affiliation 60, 66, 70, 77, 88, 105, 106, 122–124
Agency 60, 66, 70, 77, 88, 122
antidepressants 9–11
anxiety 2, 15, 16, 30, 31, 36, 37
avoidance 2, 3, 8, 16, 21, 25, 37, 71, 83, 109

behavioral activation 20, 34, 84, 89

case examples 74–78, 101–109
causal theory conclusions 17–20 *see also* Transference Hypothesis
CBASP model 2–3, 13, 26, 89
complementary 36, 60, 68–71, 88
consequences 3–6, 18–21, 28, 37, 65
Contingent Personal Responsivity 8, 23, 58, 68, 74–78 *see also* Disciplined Personal Involvement
coping strategies 18, 19, 25, 26, 36, 37, 66, 70, 71, 80, 105, 108
Coping Survey Questionnaire 20, 35, 39, 44, 110–118 *see also* Situational Analysis
cycle of depression 34, 36, 38, 39

defeatist thinking 8, 36, 37, 71, 81
Depression Timeline 27, 29, 30
Desired Outcome 7, 48, 51, 70, 71, 87, 116–118
Disciplined Personal Involvement 8, 15, 19, 21, 24, 55, 58, 75 *see also* Contingent Personal Responsivity; Interpersonal Discrimination Exercise
disclosure 22, 54, 55, 71, 101
dysthymia 1, 27, 29, 37, 93

early-onset 2, 6, 37, 84
Elicitation Phase (of Situational Analysis) 20, 24, 39–43, 52, 58

felt emotional safety 7, 15, 83, 85, 86, 119
Future Situational Analysis 47, 51, 117

global thinking 18, 25, 36, 37, 39, 71, 77, 85
grounded 19, 48, 50, 118

hidden motives 66, 68, 78
hopelessness 3, 4, 20, 25, 30, 35–38, 85

Impact Message Inventory 23, 87–89
Interpersonal Circumplex 23–26, 59–63, 65, 66, 70, 71, 87–89, 105–107, 122–124
Interpersonal Discrimination Exercise 8, 22, 23, 58, 85, 119 *see also* Disciplined Personal Involvement
interpersonal dispositions 25, 36, 61, 87–90, 104
interpersonal domain 16, 18–20, 22, 31–33, 53–55, 57, 71, 80, 86, 101–104 *see also* Transference Hypothesis
interpersonal efficacy 123, 124
interpersonal impact 6, 18, 54, 55, 63, 64, 87, 88
interpersonal motives 4, 8, 60, 66, 68–71, 80, 88
interpersonal problems 20, 36, 60, 63–66, 69–71, 89, 104, 107
interpersonal profile 66, 67, 70, 73, 80
interpersonal style *see* interpersonal dispositions
interpersonal values 59, 60, 63, 64, 80, 89, 104, 105, 123, 124
interpretation 40, 45, 50, 77, 110, 113, 117, 118, 120, 121 *see also* Action Interpretation
intimacy 16, 22, 55, 71, 99–101
isolation 21, 26, 32, 37, 70, 85, 109

134 INDEX

late-onset 2–4

major depression 1, 2, 14, 27–29, 36, 84, 92, 93
Major Depressive Disorder *see* major depression
making mistakes 18, 22, 55, 77–78, 99–101
medication 5, 9–11, 15, 25–27, 29, 84
Mood Chart 27, 29, 94

negative emotions 22, 32, 36, 41, 71, 74, 76, 104
non-complimentary 60, 68–71

perceived functionality 4, 7, 21, 51, 83, 87
persistent depression 1, 2–9, 27–34, 36–39
Personal Questionnaire 17, 18, 20, 32, 54, 86,
    99–101, 104, 108
pleasure 31, 34, 36, 92
powerlessness 20, 35, 37, 38, 41, 77
preoperational 2, 23
problem-solving 6,7, 15, 16, 20, 39, 82, 83, 121

Remediation Phase (of Situational Analysis) 24,
    39, 47–50, 52, 58, 59, 118, 120–124
research 5, 6, 9, 10, 14

Significant Other History 16–20, 56
Situational Analysis 8, 20, 35, 39, 44, 47, 48,
    50–53, 58, 59, 79, 82, 109–120 *see also*
    Coping Survey Questionnaire
slice of time 8, 20, 39, 40–42, 48, 49, 70, 71, 76,
    121
social functioning 6, 13, 16, 21, 31, 71, 92
submissive 3, 4, 26, 36, 37, 63, 74, 87–89, 102,
    104, 106, 124

training 15, 16
Transference Hypothesis 16–20, 32–34, 54–57
    see also causal theory conclusions